As Morning Breaks and Evening Sets

As Morning Breaks and Evening Sets

Liturgical Prayer Services
for Ordinary and Extraordinary Events
in the Lives of Young People

Tony Alonso, Laurie Delgatto, Robert Feduccia

Saint Mary's Press™

Genuine recycled paper with 10% post-consumer waste. Printed with soy-based ink. 5078000

The publishing team included Virginia Halbur, development editor; Mary Koehler, permissions editor; Mary Duerson, copy editor; Lynn Riska, typesetter; Jonathan Thomas Goebel, designer; Andy Palmer, art director; cover photo from Digital Vision, Ltd.; manufacturing coordinated by the production services department of Saint Mary's Press.

Printed in the United States of America

Printing: 9 8 7 6 5 4 3 2 1

Year: 2012 11 10 09 08 07 06 05 04

ISBN 0-88489-810-5

Library of Congress Cataloging-in-Publication Data

Alonso, Tony
    As morning breaks and evening sets : liturgical prayer services for ordinary and extraordinary events in the lives of young people / Tony Alonso, Laurie Delgatto, and Robert Feduccia.
        p. cm.
Includes indexes.
ISBN 0-88489-810-5 (pbk.)
    1. Catholic youth-Prayer-books and devotions-English. 2. Morning prayer (Divine office)—Catholic Church—Texts. 3. Vespers—Catholic Church—Texts.
I. Delgatto, Laurie. II. Feduccia, Robert. III. Title.
BX2150.A47 2004
264'.024—dc22
                                                                      2004008847

Contents

Appendix

Indexes

Introduction

For many Roman Catholics, mentioning the Liturgy of the Hours might conjure up images of robed monks or chanting in a far-off monastery. The most familiar communal prayer for most of us is the Sunday Eucharist, the very source of our Catholic identity. This may be the only liturgical prayer some Catholics experience in their lives. But the Liturgy of the Hours is the daily prayer of the whole Church. In its balance of ritual and simplicity, song and silence, it forms us in what it means to pray regularly as a community, and it prepares us for the Sunday Eucharist.

As Morning Breaks and Evening Sets is a tool for unearthing, dusting off, and tapping into the treasures of this ancient form of prayer, but in ways that are contemporary in style and relevant to young people. In stark contrast to the belief that youth ministers require nothing less than a light show, a smoke machine, and a rock band to reach teenagers' souls, more and more youth have actually been moving toward depth and quiet and away from constant motion and noise. They are exploring ancient spiritual practices and realizing the treasures of their own faith tradition.

This resource provides an introduction to the Liturgy of the Hours, a rich and time-tested way for Christians to pray with their community of faith. This type of prayer immerses believers in the word of God found in the psalms, canticles, and scriptural readings of the Church's Tradition. *As Morning Breaks and Evening Sets* offers an introduction to this type of prayer for those who work with

young people and explains how to do it. Included in this introduction is a brief history of the Liturgy of the Hours and guidance on how to prepare and implement these services in a youth ministry or high school setting.

At the core of this project are the prayer services, which serve to embody the wisdom of Tradition in a very accessible form. They address some significant events in the lives of young people and can be used in a variety of situations, from celebrating the opening of a new school year to helping youth mourn the loss of a classmate, teacher, or youth minister. The settings can vary from a Confirmation retreat to a summer mission trip—wherever youth are gathered. Whether formal or informal, these services are intended to connect real-life experiences with the rich prayer tradition of the Church. The services are brief (20 to 30 minutes), easy to use, and fully Catholic in content and format. They will, however, require some thoughtful preparation.

Music Feature

A special music collection called *As Morning Breaks and Evening Sets: Psalms, Canticles, and Hymns for the Liturgy of the Hours* (Chicago: GIA Publications, 2004) was written specifically to be used in connection with this book. It offers wonderful, new contemporary musical settings from three of today's top liturgical composers: Tony Alonso, Michael

Mahler, and Lori True. These musical settings correspond to the psalms and canticles referred to throughout this book. Both the music collection (G-6401) and a compact disc recording (CD-609) are available through GIA Publications *(www.gia-music.com)*. Although musical renditions for many of the psalms and canticles are found in parish hymnals and may likewise be used with this book, we encourage the use of these specially chosen compositions during prayer and the use of the corresponding recording as a demonstration for performance as well as personal prayer.

Communities are encouraged to use music that is familiar so that everyone is able to participate fully. However, the companion piece mentioned previously that's published by GIA Publications offers psalms and canticles that may be difficult to find elsewhere. The settings are accessible to groups of varying resources and instrumentation. In addition to the music collection, a CD of all the songs is also available. It may be particularly helpful in parishes and schools with limited musical resources. We encourage you to use this special collection of music as you implement the services in this manual.

Overview of the Liturgy of the Hours

As Christians we are the spiritual daughters and sons of Abraham and Sarah, Isaac and Rebekah, and Jacob and Rachel. With the Jewish people, we share a common faith in the one God, and we share common Scriptures in the Old Testament. This sharing is part of our inheritance from the people of Israel. Likewise we have inherited a pattern of worship that serves as the roots for the Liturgy of the Hours.

Central to the prayer life of Jews during Jesus' time was the recitation of the Shema (Deut. 6:4–5), both in the morning and in the evening. The recitation of the Shema was not a mere recollection of these two verses of Scripture. Rather it included a remembrance of the Ten Commandments, prayers of thanksgiving, and a remembrance of God's faithfulness during the Exodus from Egyptian slavery.

It was a structured prayer that corresponded to the two daily sacrifices in the Temple in Jerusalem that occurred in the morning and in the evening. The Scriptures indicate that Jesus also prayed in this manner as a faithful Jew.

Even though the content of the prayer changed from the Jewish prayer to the Christian expression, the early Church held on to these fixed times for prayer. Later, as the Church grew, while the celebration of the Eucharist was reserved for Sunday, the faithful gathered daily at the bishop's church, his cathedral, for the singing of hymns and psalms in a more structured manner at specific hours of the day. Those times of prayer became known as the cathedral hours and took shape as ritual for offering a sacrifice of praise to God.

In the cathedral hours of the faithful, the rising of the sun was seen as a symbol of Christ, as was the lighting of candles for evensong. With such a devotion to the symbol of light, Psalm 63 became part of morning praise, and Psalm 141 became part of evensong. Psalm 63 speaks of seeking and pining for God. The Church recognized this psalm as a morning plea to pursue the Lord throughout the day, and Psalm 141 speaks of prayer as an evening sacrifice. For that reason, the authors of this resource have chosen these psalms as the primary psalms for these prayer services. As part of the sacrifice of praise, other psalms and hymns appropriate to the time of day found their way into the liturgy, in addition to Scripture readings, responses, canticles, and intercessory prayer. Eventually a sophisticated ritual for both morning praise and evensong emerged in the cathedrals.

At the Second Vatican Council, the Church emphasized that the Liturgy of the Hours is to be celebrated faithfully so as to sanctify the day. *As Morning Breaks and Evening Sets* hopes to fulfill the intention of the council. It hopes to take the ordinary and extraordinary events in the lives of young people and grieve with them, rejoice with them, intercede with them, and offer praise with them so that their lives may be sacrifices of praise in union with the whole Church.

The Structure of the Liturgy of the Hours

The Liturgy of the Hours is structured in the following pattern:

- invocation
- hymn
- psalmody
- reading from the Scriptures
- response to the reading
- Gospel canticle
- intercessions
- dismissal

All liturgical prayer follows this pattern of dialogue. The Liturgy of the Hours is no exception. The presider calls us to prayer in the invocation, and the hymn brings together the many different voices into one. As communal prayer, it is vital to an authentic experience of prayer that the faithful gathered be forged as one body in Christ. The hymn serves that function.

Gathered as one body, the faithful offer a sacrifice of praise to God. In the Eucharistic celebration, the People of God offer the gifts of bread and wine. Likewise, the psalms as the inspired word of God are gifts from God offered back to God. The psalms are words of perfect praise to the Lord and constitute a perfect sacrifice of praise.

This dialogue with God continues as the word of God is proclaimed in the Scriptures and the faithful respond as a community. After the response to the Scripture readings, the faithful pray the Gospel canticle.

As morning praise and evensong are the hinges upon which the day turns, the Gospel canticles are hinges upon which the entire liturgies turn. In the morning, the Canticle of Zechariah is sung as a hymn to God's faithfulness, faithfulness that has seen us through the night into the light of a new day. In the evening, we sing the Canticle of Mary as a hymn to God's providence and justice. Throughout the day, we have seen God's word go out and bear fruit. The hungry are filled, the lowly are raised high, and God has helped the people.

After the canticle, the people are invited to bring their needs before the Lord. God's care for us invites us to ask: What are the needs of the Church, the world, and the community? What are our needs? All our prayers and petitions then culminate as we pray the perfect prayer, the Lord's Prayer. Finally, just as in the Eucharistic celebration, we are sent forth from our worship to live in the light and to bear the light of Christ to a world plagued by shadows.

To Sing or Not to Sing?

The authors of this resource hope the richness of the Liturgy of the Hours is made available to young people. Because of the unique situation of each parish and school, it is important to remember that the prayer services in this book should be adapted to meet your distinctive needs. Keep in mind though that to be faithful to the Liturgy of the Hours, the official prayer of the Church, these services need to be both communal and musical.

The Liturgy of the Hours is not the prayer of the individual. Rather, it is the prayer of the entire Body of Christ. Even though those who commit to praying the Liturgy of the Hours daily (deacons, priests, and bishops) most likely pray the Liturgy of the Hours privately, it does not take away from the prayer's communal nature. By praying at morning and evening, they join with others who are also praying at that moment. Although separated by distance, those who pray the Liturgy of the Hours are never alone. Other voices are praying with them.

The psalms and canticles in the Liturgy of the Hours are meant to be sung. At the praying of the Liturgy of the Hours, if at all possible, try to have present cantors capable of leading the assembly in melodic praise and musicians able to play skillfully. If that isn't possible, the music collection to be used in tandem with this book, *As Morning Breaks and Evening Sets: Psalms, Canticles, and Hymns for the Liturgy of the Hours,* can be a helpful resource (see page 9).

If the psalms and canticles are to be proclaimed in spoken word rather than sung, maintain a musical sense even in the absence of a cantor or musicians. The psalms and canticles have inherent rhythm. The psalmist can help to reveal that rhythm by proclaiming the verses of the psalm and inviting the assembly to respond after each stanza with a line from the psalm used as a refrain. Or you may choose to have the presider and the assembly take turns reciting the stanzas. Another option is to divide the assembly into two groups and take turns reciting the stanzas. Although these approaches are not melodic, such back-and-forth recitations of the psalms and canticles are musical in their rhythm. Rhythmic translations of the psalms can be found in *Christian Prayer: The Liturgy of the Hours* (New York: Catholic Book Publishing Co.,

1976). You can also find various translations in an electronic format (see page 118 for a list of Web sites). The text for the canticles using this format can be found in the appendix.

Ministers of Prayer

As in all liturgical prayer, the role of the assembly is the most important one. Without the assembly there could be no liturgy. However, various ministers are needed to fulfill specific roles. This section includes descriptions of the ministries and how to prepare people to participate in each of them. Again, remember to keep in mind the resources of your parish or school. In their fullness, the prayer services in this book can involve all of the different ministries listed, but in some situations you may be able to enlist only a presider, a reader, and a psalmist.

The Presider

The presider will need the most preparation. He or she proclaims the prayers, sings the psalms, and experiences the silences as part of the assembly, but in a way that engages everyone else's participation. He or she determines the pacing of the prayer, especially the silences, and therefore needs to be extremely familiar with the structure of the prayer service. The presider should never be looking ahead in the script for what comes next but needs to know the rhythm of the entire prayer by heart. The presider must also know the prayers well, having practiced them silently and aloud several times before the service. With time and experience comes the grace and skill of a strong presider. Spend time in the worship space with the presider, reviewing even the smallest details of choreography and proclamation. A liturgy director or a priest also may be able to offer some guidance to the presider in his or her preparation.

The Reader

The reader who proclaims the Scripture reading needs to know her or his reading inside and out. She or he must spend time reflecting on the reading alone or with others, getting to know its historical context, and practicing it aloud. After the

person assigned to read has had adequate time to prepare alone, let her or him practice the reading aloud for you in the worship space. Work on pacing, diction, and eye contact. When multiple readers are used for a reading, it is important that they rehearse together several times so that the use of multiple readers enhances the reading rather than detracts from it.

The Cantor

As in the Sunday Eucharist, the cantor has a crucial role in the Liturgy of the Hours. The cantor is the person who leads all prayer that is sung. More than just knowing the songs, the cantor needs to be comfortable with gestures and facial expressions that invite the entire assembly into participating in the gathering and gathering song, canticle, and other sung responses. Cantoring may be a difficult skill for people who are accustomed to performing *for* others. The cantor's primary task is to allow the entire assembly to "perform" for God. Make sure the cantor's gestures, relationship to the microphone, and knowledge of the music reflects an engaging dialogue between him or her and the assembly.

The Psalmist

The psalmist proclaims the sung psalm and invites the assembly's response with her or his gesture. The psalmist's role is similar to that of a lector, but is proclaiming the Scriptures in song rather than in spoken word. If your school or parish is small and has a limited supply of vocalists, you may need to have the psalmist lead a spoken version of the psalms. But if you have many talented singers, a good way to involve one or two of them (if two psalms will be used) is to include a psalmist capable of proclaiming the psalm in song in addition to a cantor.

The psalmist, like the reader, needs to know the psalm in its biblical context and its relationship to the liturgy. He or she needs to pray or sing the words many times before proclaiming it for the assembly. Through the psalmist's proclamation of the psalm, he or she should be able to convey the psalm in a way that shows strong preparation and understanding of the poetry. Like the cantor, he or she must also remember that the invitation of the assembly to sing its part (or respond in spoken word) is as important as the parts that he or she will proclaim alone.

The Choir

Although you may invite singers to support the assembly's singing, don't emphasize their role, especially in smaller settings. If you use a choir, consider placing them in the midst of the assembly. Having well-prepared, strong singers encourages everyone to participate.

Instrumentalists

The support of talented instrumentalists can greatly enhance any prayer service. The key is to prepare the instrumentalists in a way that emphasizes that their role in leading the assembly's sung prayer requires a different set of skills than does other types of playing. Teach them when it is appropriate to play and when it is not, that their ministry is at the service of the assembly and the song. This takes practice and patience. Also, take care to monitor the volume of the instruments in relationship to one another and the assembly so that the instrumentalists don't overpower the assembly's voice.

The Person Offering the Reflection

If you are including a reflection, it is important that the person who offers it can handle the responsibility. It is also essential that you work with her or him to prepare and that you approve the final draft so that it is theologically and pastorally appropriate. A good way to begin the process is to break open the word with a few young people and the person who will give the reflection. If you are not comfortable with this role, your parish priest or campus minister may be able to help. More information on how to prepare a reflection can be found on pages 116–117 of this manual.

Discerning Roles

Everyone has different gifts. Sometimes it may be necessary to encourage a young person to share a special talent or skill. Other times you may need to help a person discern a ministry that is best suited to his or her skills when one is not obvious. Besides participating in the ministries mentioned in the steps that follow, people can help plan the services, create the art and environment, write the prayers, and greet people as they enter the worship space. No matter how big or small the ministry is, make sure the ministers are clear about their roles as both servants to and part of the assembly.

Take enough time to familiarize the young people with their roles and to make sure they are comfortable with what they are doing. The amount of time you spend preparing them will reflect the importance of doing this ministry well.

Planning a Prayer Service with Young People

The Liturgy of the Hours is the sustained, formal, yet nonsacramental prayer of the Church. The Constitution on the Sacred Liturgy stresses the redemptive power of the liturgy and the importance of active participation. This is especially true of the Eucharistic celebration but encompasses all liturgical prayer, particularly the Liturgy of the Hours. In light of this, take great care in planning it. Below are a few things to keep in mind when planning to use the services in this book. Additional information on planning prayer services can be found in the appendix.

Step 1. Assemble a team. At its root, *liturgy* means "the work of the people." Make it the people's prayer. Gather a small group of young people who will lead the planning of the prayer. Be sure to include someone who is able to represent the musicians well. As you get into the planning, you may discover a particular piece of music fits the occasion. If so, make sure it is a piece that the musicians are comfortable with.

Step 2. Set the agenda for the first meeting. You are choosing to use this resource for prayer because you are celebrating a particular event. In order to plan effectively, answer *who, what, when,* and *where*:

- **Who will be gathered, and who will be ministering?** We must minister to those who gather, not to those who do the gathering. What songs are they familiar with? Do they have any favorites? Would any particular symbols speak to them? What songs are the musicians and cantor comfortable with? Who should preside or read?

- **What is the event?** What is the mood of the group likely to be? Which of the services best articulates the prayer of the group? What do the young people need to hear from God or say to God from their hearts about the event? In order to authentically speak to and hear from the Lord, you will need the pulse of the group.
- **When is the prayer service to occur?** During which liturgical season will the prayer be prayed? To be authentic to the intention of the Liturgy of the Hours, prayer during Easter should express the Resurrection, as opposed to Lent's focus on the cross. What time of day will the prayer service take place? The psalms and the canticles are dependent on the time of day. Also, if the service is prayed in the evening, you may need to address special needs, such as lighting for the presider, the reader, and the musicians if the room lighting will be dimmed.
- **Where will the people gather?** Will there be enough space to accommodate everyone? Is the space too large to maintain an intimate feel? Are there enough hymnals and resources in the space?

Bringing up such questions at the first meeting will help provide a prayerful experience for both the leaders and the participants. Be sure to designate who is responsible for assembling the musicians, setting the art and the environment, and providing all of the necessary print materials for the leaders and the assembly.

Step 3. Choose your leaders. Make sure you choose leaders who are capable of doing the task. Some young people are comfortable in front of people. Others are not. Regardless of their natural ability, empower the young people for success. Provide the presider with the order and text of worship well in advance and, if possible, rehearse with her or him in the worship space. Be sure the reader has the reading and the opportunity to rehearse in the worship space. Likewise, all those involved with the music—the choir, the instrumentalists, the cantor, and the psalmist—should have their music before the first practice. They will need time to practice as a group in the worship space.

Step 4. Invite the participants. If you are in a school, it will be easy to announce the prayer service. However, if you are in another setting, be sure to allow time for people to make plans.

Step 5. Secure any materials. Check in with the people responsible for art, environment, and any printed materials. Everything should be ready to go the day before.

Step 6. Pray. Don't let the busyness of planning a prayer service distract from your own need for prayer.

Some Final Thoughts

Take time with this manual before implementing these services. Get to know the history of the Liturgy of the Hours and its structure. That will enable you to begin to implement the prayer services with a strong understanding of the elements that make up morning and evening prayer. Work with the music director to find music that the young people will know. Spend time with the young people preparing them for their ministry. Investing a significant amount of time to beginning to pray this way will pay off in many ways as your community makes this prayer its own. Most important, trust that the gifts and spirituality of the young people you serve are as incredible as they are varied.

For the Liturgy of the Hours to truly reach its full potential as a way of prayer, it needs to be done regularly and to happen gradually. Begin with special occasions, using the topics in this book as potential opportunities to pray together. Work toward seasonal, monthly, then weekly prayer services. Soon the morning and evening prayer of the Church will become an integrated part of your ministry with young people. In time you will find yourself planning liturgies with young people and adapting them in length and content to the circumstances of the occasion.

Prayer Services for Ordinary and Extraordinary Events

In Times of Newness

IN THE CONTEXT OF MORNING PRAYER

Overview

This prayer service celebrates the blessing of newness in the lives of young people. It provides an opportunity to celebrate and reflect on the possibilities and joy that come with the beginning of a new year, a new school year, a new member of the group, or simply a new day. This prayer service would be especially appropriate for Morning Prayer during the Easter Season, when we celebrate fifty days of pure joy and delight in a God who makes all things new.

Preparation

Guide for Preparing a Reflection

If you are including a reflection after the Scripture reading, Revelation 21:1–5, give a copy of the following guide to the person who will be leading it and suggest that he or she adapt it to his or her own style and purpose:

> God is good, all the time! The Bible begins with the Genesis story of Creation, recounting God's creation of the world as being something "very good." The Bible ends with the same vision in this passage from Revelation: a glimpse of the good that is still to come as we look forward to the great homecoming feast in heaven. This vision of the Reign of God wakes us up to the fact that it is something that can be celebrated in the present. Every new day presents the opportunity to experience the newness of life and to get glimpses of the Reign of God on earth. How can we touch the Reign of God each day? What opportunities do new experiences provide us with? How can we make the best out of newness in our lives? How open are we to letting God renew us each day?

Preparing the Music

When choosing the gathering song for this service, choose something that is familiar to all so that everyone can easily join in singing. The following selections can be found in the second edition of *Gather Comprehensive*, published by GIA Publications:

- "All Things New," by Rory Cooney
- "Send Us Your Spirit," by David Haas
- "Fresh as the Morning," by Tony Alonso
- "Christ Is Alive," by Lori True and Brian Wren
- "Sing a New Song," by Dan Schutte

Order of Prayer: In Times of Newness

All the prayers in this service are led by the presider unless otherwise indicated.

Gathering Song

The person leading song stands, motions for all to stand, and invites the assembly to join in the gathering song.

At the conclusion of the song, all sit. If necessary, the presider motions for all to sit.

Psalmody

After all are seated, without rushing, the cantor or the choir begins the first psalm. The cantor or the choir sings the verses, and the assembly sings the response. If the psalms are proclaimed, the responses can be used after each verse.

First Psalm: Psalm 63

[*All respond.*] "As morning breaks I look to you; I look to you, O Lord, to be my strength this day" (*Gather Comprehensive*).

After a brief period of silence following the conclusion of the psalm, the presider stands and motions for all to stand, and she or he proclaims the psalm prayer.

Psalm Prayer

> Let us pray. [*Pause.*]
> God of all creation,
> source of all light and life,
> as morning breaks,
> we sing our praise and thanks to you
> for the wonder and beauty
> of this new day.
> May our prayer glorify
> your holy name

and our work this day
be an offering to you.
We ask this through Christ, our Lord.

[All respond.] Amen.

After the psalm prayer, the presider motions for all to sit. Without rushing, the cantor or the choir begins the second psalm.

Second Psalm: Psalm 66

[All respond.] "Let all the earth cry out in joy to the Lord" (*Gather Comprehensive*).

After a brief period of silence following the conclusion of the psalm, the presider stands and motions for all to stand, and he or she proclaims the psalm prayer.

Psalm Prayer

Let us pray. *[Pause.]*
God of life,
we cry out in joy to you
for the glory of each new breath we take,
and for the blessings of your
relentless love in our lives.
As we call upon you,
on this new day,
lead us from death to new life,
in Christ Jesus, your Son and our Lord.

[All respond.] Amen.

After the psalm prayer, the presider motions for all to sit. Without rushing, the reader or readers stand to proclaim the reading from the Scriptures.

Scripture Reading:
Revelation 21:1–5

A reading from the Book of Revelation:

Then I saw a new heaven and a new earth; for the first heaven and the first earth had passed away, and the sea was no more. And I saw the holy city, the new Jerusalem, coming down out of heaven from God, prepared as a bride adorned for her husband. And I heard a loud voice from the throne saying,

"See, the home of God is among mortals.
He will dwell with them;
they will be his peoples,
and God himself will be with them;
he will wipe every tear from their eyes.
Death will be no more;
mourning and crying and pain will be no more,
for the first things have passed away."

And the one who was seated on the throne said, "See, I am making all things new."

The word of the Lord.

[All respond.] Thanks be to God.

Optional Reflection

After the reading, observe a period of silence. If there is to be a reflection, the person giving it stands. If there is no reflection, after the silence, all stand for the canticle.

Canticle

As the cantor begins the Canticle of Zechariah (the Benedictus), the presider and all make the sign of the cross. If this is to be read, see page 120 for a copy of the text.

Intercessions

All remain standing as the presider invites the assembly to pray the intercessions. After the reader has led the petitions, the presider concludes by offering a final prayer of petition:

Let us place our needs before God, who makes all things new, as we say, *Lord, let your face shine on us.*

- For open eyes and hearts to the blessings of each new day and new experience, we pray, . . . *[all respond]* Lord, let your face shine on us.
- For courage to accept new things in our lives, in times of joy and in times of sorrow, we pray, . . . *[all respond]* Lord, let your face shine on us.
- For renewed energy for all those who serve as teachers and mentors to students of all ages, we pray, . . . *[all respond]* Lord, let your face shine on us.
- For relief and comfort for all those who suffer in body, mind, and spirit, especially for those we now mention aloud *[mention names]*, we pray, . . . *[all respond]* Lord, let your face shine on us.

- For all those who have gone on to the new and eternal Jerusalem, for lasting peace and eternal joy, especially *[mention names]*, we pray, . . . *[all respond]* Lord, let your face shine on us.
- For the prayers we hold in our hearts and those we offer aloud *[pause for prayers offered by the community]*, we pray, . . . *[all respond]* Lord, let your face shine on us.

God of abundance, hear our prayers
and grant us each day the newness of your love
and the beauty of your grace.
We ask this through Christ, our risen Lord.

[All respond.] Amen.

Closing Prayer and Blessing

The following prayer and blessing are led by the presider:

The Lord's Prayer

As baptized people thankful for the blessings of this new day, let us pray the prayer Christ himself taught us. *[All join in.]* Our Father . . .

Closing Blessing

Let us bow our heads and pray for God's blessing:
May the joy of knowing
God's unending love
guide our steps in ways of peace
this day and always.

[All respond.] Amen.

And may almighty God bless us,
Father, Son, and Holy Spirit.

[All respond.] Amen.

Sign of Peace

My sisters and brothers, let us go forth sharing with one another a sign of Christ's peace.

In Times of Crisis

IN THE CONTEXT OF EVENING PRAYER

Overview

This prayer service provides an opportunity for prayer and communal support during times of crisis. It may be used when an unexpected death occurs, in the aftermath of a natural disaster (such as a hurricane, a fire, a tornado, or an earthquake), during times of civil unrest, or in times of terrorism. It is also appropriate when a community is experiencing the loss of industry and jobs or when harm has been done to an individual or a community (such as from a school shooting, looting, or violence). Whatever the situation, the service offers the participants an opportunity to pray for and about a crisis or its aftermath.

Preparation

Guide for Preparing a Reflection

If you are including a reflection after the Scripture reading, Romans 8:35,37–39, give a copy of the following guide to the person who will be leading it and suggest that she or he adapt it to her or his own style and purpose:

> The events of our lives, especially the painful and difficult ones, stay with us forever. All our experiences become a part of the fabric of our lives and offer opportunity for growth. But we have a choice: to grow through such events or to

be hardened by them. What has happened is not something to be gotten over. It is not something to forget and put behind us. It is something we learn to live through, and we carry the lessons with us into the future. God's invitation in these events is to trust that God will sustain our lives under any circumstances. This time is not comfortable—quite the opposite. But it is the quintessential teaching moment.

> To trust is to recognize that Christ is in our midst, healing us, transforming us, renewing us, and guiding us. Nothing separates us from God. Trust in the Lord, who misses nothing that happens in our lives, who has the power to bring joy out of sorrow, wholeness out of brokenness, and hope out of despair.

Preparing the Music

When choosing the gathering song for this service, choose something that is familiar to all so that everyone can easily join in singing. The following selections can be found in the second edition of *Gather Comprehensive*, published by GIA Publications:

- "Neither Death Nor Life," by Marty Haugen
- "Why Stand So Far Away, My God?" by Michael Mahler and Ruth Duck
- "The Cloud's Veil," by Liam Lawton
- "O God, Why Are You Silent?" by Marty Haugen
- "I Heard the Voice of Jesus Say" (traditional English)

Order of Prayer: In Times of Crisis

All the prayers in this service are led by the presider unless otherwise indicated.

Gathering Song

The presider stands and motions for all to stand. The person leading song invites the assembly to join in singing the gathering song.

At the conclusion of the song, all sit. If necessary, the presider motions for all to sit.

Psalmody

After all are seated, without rushing, the cantor or the choir begins the first psalm. The cantor or the choir sings the verses, and the assembly sings the response. If the psalms are proclaimed, the responses can be used after each verse.

First Psalm: Psalm 141

[All respond.] "Let my prayer rise before you like incense, O Lord, and my hands like an evening off'ring" *(Gather Comprehensive)*.

After a brief period of silence following the conclusion of the psalm, the presider stands and motions for all to stand, and she or he proclaims the psalm prayer.

Psalm Prayer

Let us pray. *[Pause.]*
Source of all love and life,
hear our voices as we cry out to you.
We call out to you,
O Lord, to fill our hearts with your Spirit,
so that as we are faced with the difficulties and anxieties
that life has brought us,
we may remember your eternal love,
and trust in the promise of your presence.

O God, our strength and stay,
our times are in your hands:
you uphold us in the chances and changes of our lives,
you do not abandon us in our distress.
Give us courage in this time of trial,
make us gracious and generous even as we suffer,
and lift our spirits that we may live always
in the confidence of your nearness and love.
We ask this through your Son,
our Lord, Jesus Christ,
in the unity of the Holy Spirit,
one God forever and ever.

[All respond.] Amen.

After the psalm prayer, the presider motions for all to sit. Without rushing, the cantor or the choir begins the second psalm.

Second Psalm: Psalm 121

[All respond.] "Our help comes from the Lord, the maker of heaven and earth" *(Gather Comprehensive).*

After a brief period of silence following the conclusion of the psalm, the presider stands and motions for all to stand, and he or she proclaims the psalm prayer.

Psalm Prayer

Let us pray. *[Pause.]*
Lord God, maker of heaven and earth,
our help comes from you and you alone.
You, O God, give meaning to our hopes,
to our struggles, and to our strivings.
Without you we are lost, our lives empty.
And so when all else fails us, we turn to you!
When in agony, we are bystanders to our own confusion.
We look to you for peace.
Give us strength to face life with hope and courage,
that even from its discord and conflicts we may draw blessings.
We believe that you will hear us
in this time of difficulty and suffering.
Help us keep the image of your Son ever before us,
and let us feel the healing calm of your embrace.

God, all-powerful, you know our pain and see our tears.
Listen to our prayer, for we know our help comes from you.
We pray this in your Son's name.

[All respond.] Amen.

After the psalm prayer, the presider motions for all to sit. Without rushing, the reader or readers stand to proclaim the reading from the Scriptures.

Scripture Reading:
Romans 8:35,37–39

A reading from the letter of Paul to the Romans:

Who will separate us from the love of Christ? Will hardship, or distress, or persecution, or famine, or nakedness, or peril, or sword? . . . No, in all these things we are more than conquerors through him who loved us. For I am convinced that neither death, nor life, nor angels, nor rulers nor things present, nor things to come, nor powers, nor heights, nor depth, nor anything else in all creation, will be able to separate us from the love of God in Christ Jesus our Lord.

The word of the Lord.

[All respond.] Thanks be to God.

Optional Reflection

After the reading, observe a period of silence. If there is to be a reflection, the person giving it stands. If there is no reflection, after the silence, all stand for the canticle.

Canticle

As the cantor begins the canticle, the presider and all make the sign of the cross.

For evening prayer, the Canticle of Mary is the standard canticle. If the prayer service is held later in the evening, the Canticle of Simeon may be used instead. If the prayer is to be read, see page 119 or 121 for a copy of the text.

Intercessions

All remain standing as the presider invites the assembly to pray the intercessions. After the reader has led the petitions, the presider concludes by offering a final prayer of petition:

Surely Christ has borne our grief and carried our sorrows. Therefore we turn to God in prayer during this time of crisis, saying, *O Christ, hear us.*

- God of the nations and all peoples, we cry to you for consolation. We pray, . . . *[all respond]* O Christ, hear us.
- God of all power, we come to you in fear. We pray, . . . *[all respond]* O Christ, hear us.
- Unshakable God, we call out to you in grief and anxiety. We pray, . . . *[all respond]* O Christ, hear us.
- All-seeing God, keep watch over all who have been harmed and those who minister to them. We pray, . . . *[all respond]* O Christ, hear us.
- Compassionate God, send your Holy Spirit to soothe the suffering and comfort the afflicted. We pray, . . . *[all respond]* O Christ, hear us.
- Ever-present God, help us to feel your nearness in the midst of this ominous day. We pray, . . . *[all respond]* O Christ, hear us.
- Welcoming God, bless the dying and receive them into the arms of your mercy. We pray, . . . *[all respond]* O Christ, hear us.
- God of blessing, support our national leaders and all who hold authority in the nations of the world. We pray, . . . *[all respond]* O Christ, hear us.
- Finally, O God of truth, work through our struggle and confusion to accomplish your purposes on earth and to unite us in harmony and love. We pray, . . . *[all respond]* O Christ, hear us.

Great God of all, have mercy and heal us.
God of love, God of truth, God of life, God of hope,
you know our needs are great at this time.
You know them better than we can even state them now.
In your mercy, hear our prayer.
In your wisdom, grant us those things
that will lead us forward to wholeness, love, and peace again.
In your grace, bless us in this time with your holy and life-giving
        presence.
For blessed are you, O God, and blessed is all that you do.

[All respond.] Amen.

Closing Prayer and Blessing

The following prayer and blessing are led by the presider:

The Lord's Prayer

As a sign of unity and reverence for one another, let us join hands and pray the perfect prayer. *[All join in.]* Our Father . . .

Closing Blessing

Let us bow our heads and pray for God's blessing:
The God of love be with us all.

[All respond.] Amen.

The Christ of grace be for us all.

[All respond.] Amen.

The Spirit of peace be among us all.

[All respond.] Amen.

Let us go forth into the world trusting the power of God's grace and love.

[All respond.] Thanks be to God.

Sign of Peace

Let us conclude our prayer by extending to one another a sign of God's peace.

In Times of Remembrance

IN THE CONTEXT OF EVENING PRAYER

Overview

This prayer service is a way of remembering, celebrating, and honoring all who have died. It could be used on the anniversary of the death of someone close to the group or as a remembrance of all friends and family members who have died. The week of All Souls' Day (*Día de los Muertos*) would be an especially appropriate time to use this service. The entire month of November has traditionally been a time to remember the dead and celebrate eternal life. Also, national holidays such as Veterans Day and Memorial Day would be appropriate times to use this service.

Preparation

Guide for Preparing a Reflection

If you are including a reflection after the scriptural reading, John 11:32–45, give a copy of the following guide to the person who will be leading it and suggest that he or she adapt it to his or her own style and purpose:

> How often do we want to cry out, like Mary: "Lord, if you had been here, my brother would not have died" (John 11:32). When Jesus arrives where everyone is mourning the

death of Lazarus, rather than offer words of explanation, he simply weeps with them and shares their pain. The tears we cry and the anger we sometimes feel when someone close to us has passed away is pain that Jesus himself felt. When we cry out to God at the loss of a loved one, the image of Jesus weeping at the death of his friend can be one of great comfort because rather than trying to offer an easy answer, it reminds us of a God whose compassion is great, who weeps with us in our grief and questioning. However, the story doesn't end there. Jesus raises Lazarus from the dead. The story doesn't end for us either because the God who raised Lazarus raises all of us. As Catholics we are a resurrection people. Even in the midst of profound sorrow and loss, we cling to the belief that we shall "see the goodness of the Lord in the land of the living" (Psalm 27:13). When we gather to remember those we have lost, even in our sorrow, we must also give thanks to God for the gift of their presence in our lives as well as for the promise that we will all be raised up on the last day.

Preparing the Music

When choosing the gathering song for this service, choose something that is familiar to all so that everyone can easily join in singing. The following selections can be found in the second edition of *Gather Comprehensive*, published by GIA Publications:

- "Litany of the Saints," by John Becker
- "I Know That My Redeemer Lives," by David Haas
- "Pues Si Vivimos/If We Are Living" (traditional Spanish)
- "Soon and Very Soon," by Andraé Crouch
- "Shall We Gather at the River," by Robert Lowry

Additional Considerations

- Set up chairs to encircle the baptismal font in the church. Invite people to bring framed pictures of those who have died to place around the font. If you cannot gather around a font, find small tables to place the pictures on. Consider using other seasonal items alongside the pictures to create an altar of the departed (for example, small pumpkins or flowers during November).

- When all have gathered for prayer, begin with the opening comment before the gathering song (if you are not gathered around a font, omit the comments noted in brackets). As the gathering song is sung, have someone in the group incense the altar of the departed as a way of honoring the dead.

- Consider using a setting of the Litany of the Saints as a gathering song, incorporating the names of people in the community who have died in the past year. Be prepared to invite the prayer participants to offer names of people they would like to include.

Order of Prayer: In Times of Remembrance

All the prayers in this service are led by the presider unless otherwise indicated.

Gathering

The presider stands and motions for all to stand. The presider says:

Peace be with you.

[All respond.] And also with you.

[Read the bracketed text only if it is appropriate to your situation.] Sisters and brothers, we gather tonight [around the font of our baptism, where we were blessed and born into eternal life] to remember our loved ones who have gone on to the other side of life. We gather to remember the many gifts of these saints in our lives and to give God thanks for the promise of eternal life. [As we begin our prayer, let us call upon the saints in glory.]

Gathering Song

The presider motions for all to join in singing the gathering song. If there is an altar of the departed, it is incensed during the singing.

At the conclusion of the song, all sit. If necessary, the presider motions for all to sit.

Psalmody

After all are seated, without rushing, the cantor or the choir begins the first psalm. The cantor or the choir sings the verses, and the assembly sings the response. If the psalms are proclaimed, the responses can be used after each verse.

First Psalm: Psalm 141

[All respond.] "Let my prayer rise before you like incense, O Lord, and my hands like an evening off'ring" *(Gather Comprehensive).*

After a brief period of silence following the conclusion of the psalm, the presider stands and motions for all to stand, and he or she proclaims the psalm prayer.

Psalm Prayer

Let us pray. *[Pause.]*
Gentle God,
Let our prayers rise
like incense before you
as we place our lives in your hands.
We turn our eyes to you to be our refuge
from the pains of emptiness and loss
and to show us the path that leads to you.
In the face of death and mourning,
hold us in love,
comfort us in our times of grieving,
and heal us with your unending grace.
We ask this through Christ, our Lord.

[All respond.] Amen.

After the psalm prayer, the presider motions for all to sit. Without rushing, the cantor or the choir begins the second psalm.

Second Psalm: Psalm 27

[All respond.] "The Lord is my light and my salvation, of whom should I be afraid?" *(Gather Comprehensive).*

After a brief period of silence following the conclusion of the psalm, the presider stands and motions for all to stand, and she or he proclaims the psalm prayer.

Psalm Prayer

Let us pray. *[Pause.]*
God, our light, our salvation,
when we surrender ourselves to you,
we fear nothing.
The goodness of your love
leads us to the land of the living.
As we place our trust in you,
open our hearts to your presence
in our praying, our singing, and our silence.

In times of grief and sadness,
we pray that you will hear our prayer
and grant us the joy of eternal life.
Hear us, as we make our prayer
through your Son, our Lord,
Jesus Christ.

[All respond.] Amen.

After the psalm prayer, the presider motions for all to sit. Without rushing, the reader or readers stand to proclaim the reading from the Scriptures.

Scripture Reading:
John 11:32–45

A reading from the holy Gospel according to John:

When Mary came where Jesus was and saw him, she knelt at his feet and said to him, "Lord, if you had been here, my brother would not have died." When Jesus saw her weeping, and the Jews who came with her also weeping, he was greatly disturbed in spirit and deeply moved. He said, "Where have you laid him?" They said to him, "Lord, come and see." Jesus began to weep. So the Jews said, "See how he loved him!" But some of them said, "Could not he who opened the eyes of the blind man have kept this man from dying?"

Then Jesus, again greatly disturbed, came to the tomb. It was a cave, and a stone was lying against it. Jesus said, "Take away the stone." Martha, the sister of the dead man, said to him, "Lord, already there is a stench because he has been dead four days." Jesus said to her, "Did I not tell you that if you believed, you would see the glory of God?" So they took away the stone. And Jesus looked upward and said, "Father, I thank you for having heard me. I knew that you always hear me, but I have said this for the sake of the crowd standing here, so that they may believe that you sent me." When he had said this, he cried out with a loud voice, "Lazarus, come out!" The dead man came out, his hands and feet bound with strips of cloth, and his face wrapped in a cloth. Jesus said to them, "Unbind him, and let him go."

Many of the Jews therefore, who had come with Mary and had seen what Jesus did, believed in him.

The word of the Lord.

[All respond.] Thanks be to God.

Optional Reflection

After the reading, observe a period of silence. If there is to be a reflection, the person giving it stands. If there is no reflection, after the silence, all stand for the canticle.

Canticle As the cantor begins the canticle, the presider and all make the sign of the cross.

For evening prayer, the Canticle of Mary is the standard canticle. If the prayer service is held later in the evening, the Canticle of Simeon may be used instead. If the prayer is to be read, see page 119 or 121 for a copy of the text.

Intercessions All remain standing as the presider invites the assembly to pray the intercessions. After the reader has led the petitions, the presider concludes by offering a final prayer of petition:

> In our need, we stand before you as resurrection people, laying our needs and our prayers before you, God of hope. Our response to each prayer will be, *Lord, let your face shine on us.*
>
> - For all who suffer the pain and emptiness of losing a loved one, for those whose faith is tested in times of sorrow, we pray, . . . *[all respond]* Lord, let your face shine on us.
> - For the faithful servants who serve God's people as doctors, nurses, and therapists. May they have renewed energy and hope, we pray, . . . *[all respond]* Lord, let your face shine on us.
> - For all who minister to the dying and the grieving through their support, prayers, and listening ears, we pray, . . . *[all respond]* Lord, let your face shine on us.
> - For those who are dying and for all those who love them and share their journey, we pray, . . . *[all respond]* Lord, let your face shine on us.
> - For the many saints and sinners, friends, and family members who have shown us the path of Christ and have gone on to eternal peace in heaven, especially all those we mention aloud *[pause for the mention of names]*, we pray, . . . *[all respond]* Lord, let your face shine on us.
>
> God of consolation,
> as we celebrate the
> goodness of your Kingdom,
> let your face shine on us
> in our pain and in our joy.
> Grant the prayers we offer,
> those spoken here and those
> we hold in the silence of our hearts
> through Christ Jesus, our Lord.

[All respond.] Amen.

Closing Prayer and Blessing

The following prayer and blessing are led by the presider:

The Lord's Prayer

> United with resurrection people everywhere, let us pray the prayer
> Christ himself taught us. *[All join in.]* Our Father . . .

Closing Blessing

> Let us pray. *[Pause.]*
> We give you thanks, O God,
> for the many people who
> have shown us your path.
> In our time of remembrance,
> we cling more firmly than ever
> to the promise of resurrection.
> Comfort us with your love,
> and hold us in your arms
> as we make our prayer, through
> Jesus Christ, our Lord.

[All respond.] Amen.

> Let us bow our heads and pray for God's blessing:
> May the peace of God,
> which surpasses all understanding,
> guard our hearts and our minds in Christ Jesus.

[All respond.] Amen.

> And may almighty God bless us,
> Father, Son, and Holy Spirit.

[All respond.] Amen.

Sign of Peace

> My sisters and brothers, let us go forth sharing a sign of Christ's
> peace with one another.

When Peace Is Needed

IN THE CONTEXT OF EVENING PRAYER

Overview

The need to pray for peace on global and personal levels is constant. In an age where we are surrounded by images of war and violence in our daily lives, this prayer service would be effective at any time during the year. It would be especially appropriate in times of war and conflict on a national or international level. But the prayer for peace also applies to the wars of violence, racism, and prejudice in our communities. The focus of this service is to pray for peace, but it is also to remind everyone gathered of their baptismal responsibility to be agents of Christ's peace in the world.

Preparation

Guide for Preparing a Reflection

If you are including a reflection after the Scripture reading, Philippians 4:4–7, give a copy of the following guide to the person who will be leading it and suggest that he or she adapt it to his or her own style and purpose:

> During Sunday liturgy (and at the conclusion of each of the prayer services in this book), those assembled share a sign of Christ's peace

with one another. This peace is a sign of commitment to one another. It is a commitment to peace in our homes, in our schools, in our nation, and in all nations, and a commitment to peace within ourselves. The reverent way we approach one another, embrace each other, and speak the words of peace to one another commits us to this call to deep peace. As individuals and as a community, we are called to embrace the Gospel that demands the work of peace.

Peace to many is the absence of work or concern, to others, the absence of war and violence. But when Saint Paul says, "Do not worry about anything" (Philippians 4:6), he is trying to soften hearts that have been desensitized to the lack of peace in our world. These words do not excuse us to a quiet complacency but instead call us to greater action and faith. We can begin by taking Paul's words to heart, by "letting our gentleness be known to all people" (adapted from verse 5). If we want to be peacemakers, we need to manifest it in all areas of our lives. We might begin each day praying for peace of mind and heart, and to act with justice in all that we do. The very prayer we speak will then become the way that we live. Without cultivating a peaceful heart, we will never be able to touch the peace of the Reign of God, and we will never be able to extend this peace to those around us. To pray for peace without constantly cultivating it in every aspect of our lives is not truly praying for peace. God needs the hands and hearts of all of us to do this unending work.

Preparing the Music

When choosing the gathering song for this service, choose something that is familiar to all so that everyone can easily join in singing. The following selections can be found in the second edition of *Gather Comprehensive*, published by GIA Publications:
- "Dona Nobis Pacem," by Taizé
- "Prayer of Peace," by David Haas
- "Give Us Your Peace," by Michael Mahler

- "World Peace Prayer," by Marty Haugen
- "Walk in the Reign," by Rory Cooney

Additional Considerations

- As people gather for prayer, consider having the instrumentalists play a repetitive mantra, like a Taizé, to gather everyone (see the section "Preparing the Music" for suggestions). Once everyone has arrived for prayer, have the cantor or the choir begin singing the refrain, inviting everyone to join in. Let the singing continue for awhile, with everyone sitting, and then continue the service with the first psalm.
- The Scripture reading is scripted for two readers. However, it could easily be done by a single reader with slight adaptation of the repeated lines.

Order of Prayer: When Peace Is Needed

All the prayers in this service are led by the presider unless otherwise indicated.

Gathering Song

The presider stands and motions for all to stand and join in singing the gathering song. See the section "Additional Considerations" for a possible alteration.

At the conclusion of the song, all sit. If necessary, the presider motions for all to sit.

Psalmody

After all are seated, without rushing, the cantor or the choir begins the first psalm. The cantor or the choir sings the verses, and the assembly sings the response. If the psalms are proclaimed, the responses can be used after each verse.

First Psalm: Psalm 141

[All respond.] "Let my prayer rise before you like incense, O Lord, and my hands like an evening off'ring" *(Gather Comprehensive)*.

After a brief period of silence following the conclusion of the psalm, the presider stands and motions for all to stand, and she or he proclaims the psalm prayer.

Psalm Prayer

> Let us pray. *[Pause.]*
> God of peace,
> Our prayers rise to you
> like incense burning in the night,
> prayers that cry for peace
> and relief from the fears that divide us.
> Come, replace our anger with compassion,
> and our prejudice with peace.

Listen to our call
and turn our eyes to you.
Give us peace and protection
and hold us close this night.
We ask this through Christ, our Lord.

[All respond.] Amen.

After the psalm prayer, the presider motions for all to sit. Without rushing, the cantor or the choir begins the second psalm.

Second Psalm: Psalm 131

[All respond.] "In you, O Lord, I have found my peace" *(Gather Comprehensive).*

After a brief period of silence following the conclusion of the psalm, the presider stands and motions for all to stand, and he or she proclaims the psalm prayer.

Psalm Prayer

Let us pray. *[Pause.]*
In you alone, O Lord,
we find everlasting peace.
Amid violence and terror,
you hold each of us like a mother
holds her child.
Stir in us a fire of
compassion that we may
serve as peacemakers in all
we say and do,
imitating the life
of your Son, our Lord,
Jesus Christ.

[All respond.] Amen.

After the psalm prayer, the presider motions for all to sit. Without rushing, the reader or readers stand to proclaim the reading from the Scriptures.

Scripture Reading:
Philippians 4:4–7

Reader 1:

A reading from the letter of Paul to the Philippians:

Reader 2:

Rejoice in the Lord always; again, I will say, Rejoice.

Reader 1:

Let your gentleness be known to everyone. The Lord is near.

Reader 2:

Do not worry about anything, but in everything by prayer and supplication with thanksgiving let your requests be made known to God.

Reader 1:

And the peace of God,

Reader 2:

[And the peace of God,]

Reader 1:

which surpasses all understanding,

Both readers:

will guard your hearts and your minds in Christ Jesus.

The word of the Lord.

[All respond.] Thanks be to God.

Optional Reflection

After the reading, observe a period of silence. If there is to be a reflection, the person giving it stands. If there is no reflection, after the silence, all stand for the canticle.

Canticle

As the cantor begins the canticle, the presider and all make the sign of the cross. For evening prayer, the Canticle of Mary is the standard canticle. If the prayer service is held later in the evening, the Canticle of Simeon may be used instead. If the prayer is to be read, see page 119 or 121 for a copy of the text.

Intercessions

All remain standing as the presider invites the assembly to pray the intercessions. After the reader has led the petitions, the presider concludes by offering a final prayer of petition.

In thanksgiving, let our prayers and requests be known to God, whose peace guards our hearts and guides us on the right path. Our response to each prayer will be, *Sun of justice, hear our prayer.* [Note: The term *Sun* is used when speaking of Christ during the Christmas season.]

- For gentleness and peace in the hearts of our school, community, and church leaders, we pray, . . . *[all respond]* Sun of justice, hear our prayer.
- For patience and love in relationships between family members, friends, and teachers, we pray, . . . *[all respond]* Sun of justice, hear our prayer.
- For peace in all countries and all peoples torn by war and violence, for an end to killing in the name of prejudice and pride, we pray, . . . *[all respond]* Sun of justice, hear our prayer.
- For comfort to all who suffer from physical or mental illness, abuse or violence, we pray, . . . *[all respond]* Sun of justice, hear our prayer.
- For eternal peace for those who have died, especially all those who have died in acts of violence or war, especially *[pause for mention of names]*, we pray, . . . *[all respond]* Sun of justice, hear our prayer.
- For the prayers and worries we hold in the silence of our hearts and those we offer aloud *[pause for offering of prayers]*, we pray, . . . *[all respond]* Sun of justice, hear our prayer.

God of compassion,
As we strive to be people of peace and love in our world,
hear and answer the prayers
we have laid before you and grant us your peace
through Christ Jesus, our Lord.

[All respond.] Amen.

Closing Prayer and Blessing

The following prayer and blessing are led by the presider:

The Lord's Prayer

United with peace-seeking people everywhere, let us pray the prayer Christ himself taught us. *[All join in.]* Our Father . . .

Closing Blessing

Let us bow our heads and pray for God's blessing:
     May the peace of God,
     which surpasses all understanding,
     guard our hearts and our minds in Christ Jesus.

[All respond.] Amen.

     And may almighty God bless us,
     Father, Son, and Holy Spirit.

[All respond.] Amen.

Sign of Peace

     My sisters and brothers, let us go forth sharing with one another a
     commitment and a sign of Christ's peace.

In Times of Anxiety and Worry

IN THE CONTEXT OF EVENING PRAYER

Overview

This prayer service would be appropriate throughout the school year at times of high stress and anxiety in the lives of young people. It would be especially useful during final exams week or during the late winter and early spring months. That is the time of year when young people are overwhelmed with making class and activity choices for the following year and when seniors are applying to and waiting for acceptance from colleges.

Preparation

Guide for Preparing a Reflection

If you are including a reflection after the Scripture reading, Matthew 6:25–34, give a copy of the following guide to the person who will be leading it and suggest that she or he adapt it to her or his own style and purpose:

> The anxiety of everyday life in contemporary culture can be overwhelming. So many seemingly important things compete for our attention and energy. Sometimes we become convinced that our worrying and anxiety can somehow help us shape the direction of one thing or another. But Jesus puts this into perspective for us by pointing to the lilies of the field and the birds of the air. They are always taken care of without any worry on their part. We must become like the lilies and the birds, to think more simply and trust more completely. Too often we delay our happiness by thinking that we will be happy when we get that new car, find a new girlfriend or boyfriend, or graduate. If we worry about tomorrow, we fail to truly acknowledge God's presence in the gift of today. This passage reminds us that God's Reign is closer than we think, and we catch glimpses of it when we simply open our hearts to it. What can we do to remind ourselves to return our thoughts to God when our hearts are restless? Worry and anxiety about the small things in life can prevent us from having the energy to pursue those things that as baptized people we are called to be—doers of love, justice, and service in our world. What keeps us from pursuing these things? What are some other signs of God's love and care that help us focus on what is important when the anxieties of life are overwhelming? The birds in the air and the lilies of the field are only two of so many things that remind us to let go of our worries and trust in the God who created us.

Preparing the Music

When choosing the gathering song for this service, choose something that is familiar to all so that everyone can easily join in singing. The following selections can be found in the second edition of *Gather Comprehensive,* published by GIA Publications:

- "Watch, O Lord," by Marty Haugen
- "Where Your Treasure Is," by Marty Haugen
- "Nada Te Turbe," by Taizé
- "Come to Me," by Michael Joncas
- "Rain Down," by Jaime Cortéz

Additional Considerations

Consider using this prayer service at the conclusion of a large youth group gathering. Near the end of the meeting, the young people could break into small groups for discussions, sharing the anxieties of the week. Select a leader from each group who will be responsible for leading his or her group to the main prayer space at a designated time. While the small groups are meeting, the ministers for prayer can gather to make any final preparations. As everyone gathers for prayer, soft instrumental music could be played by one or more of the young people with musical skills. When all of the groups have entered and everyone is in place, the instrumental music draws to a close, the presider silently motions for all to rise, and the prayer service begins.

Order of Prayer: In Times of Anxiety and Worry

All the prayers in this service are led by the presider unless otherwise indicated.

Gathering Song

The presider stands and motions for all to stand. The person leading song invites the assembly to join in singing the gathering song.

At the conclusion of the song, all sit. If necessary, the presider motions for all to sit.

Psalmody

After all are seated, without rushing, the cantor or the choir begins the first psalm. The cantor or the choir sings the verses, and the assembly sings the response. If the psalms are proclaimed, the responses can be used after each verse.

First Psalm: Psalm 141

[All respond.] "Let my prayer rise before you like incense, O Lord, and my hands like an evening off'ring" *(Gather Comprehensive)*.

After a brief period of silence following the conclusion of the psalm, the presider stands and motions for all to stand, and he or she proclaims the psalm prayer.

Psalm Prayer

> Let us pray. *[Pause.]*
> Gentle God,
> We raise our prayers,
> worries, and hopes
> before you like incense,
> burning in the night.

As we lift our prayers to you,
kindle in us the flame of
your love that guides us
to true peace in
Christ Jesus, our Lord.

[All respond.] Amen.

After the psalm prayer, the presider motions for all to sit. Without rushing, the cantor or the choir begins the second psalm.

Second Psalm: Psalm 27

[All respond.] "The Lord is my light and my salvation, of whom should I be afraid?" *(Gather Comprehensive).*

After a brief period of silence following the conclusion of the psalm, the presider stands and motions for all to stand, and she or he proclaims the psalm prayer.

Psalm Prayer

Let us pray. *[Pause.]*
You, Lord, are our light and our salvation,
with you we fear nothing.
Your promise to lead us
to the land of the living
gives us joy and hope,
especially when our hearts
are in need of comfort,
and our minds are in need of peace.
Grant us the goodness of your grace.
We ask this through Christ Jesus, our Lord.

[All respond.] Amen.

After the psalm prayer, the presider motions for all to sit. Without rushing, the reader or readers stand to proclaim the reading from the Scriptures.

Scripture Reading:
Matthew 6:25–34

A reading from the holy Gospel according to Matthew:

"Therefore I tell you, do not worry about your life, what you will eat or what you will drink, or about your body, what you will wear. Is not life more than food, and the body more than clothing? Look at the birds of the air; they neither sow nor reap nor gather into barns, and yet your heavenly Father feeds them. Are you not of more value than they? And can any of you by worrying add a single hour to your span of life? And why do you worry about clothing? Consider the lilies of the field, how they grow; they neither toil nor spin, yet I tell you, even Solomon in all his glory was not clothed like one of these. But if God so clothes the grass of the field, which is alive today and tomorrow is thrown into the oven, will he not much more clothe you—you of little faith? Therefore do not worry, saying, 'What will we eat?' or 'What will we drink?' or 'What will we wear?' For it is the Gentiles who strive for all these things; and indeed your heavenly Father knows that you need all these things. But strive first for the kingdom of God and his righteousness, and all these things will be given to you as well.

"So do not worry about tomorrow, for tomorrow will bring worries of its own. Today's trouble is enough for today."

The word of the Lord.

[All respond.] Thanks be to God.

Optional Reflection

After the reading, observe a period of silence. If there is to be a reflection, the person giving it stands. If there is no reflection, after the silence, all stand for the canticle.

Canticle

As the cantor begins the canticle, the presider and all make the sign of the cross.

For evening prayer, the Canticle of Mary is the standard canticle. If the prayer service is held later in the evening, the Canticle of Simeon may be used instead. If the prayer is to be read, see page 119 or 121 for a copy of the text.

Intercessions

All remain standing as the presider invites the assembly to pray the intercessions. After the reader has led the petitions, the presider concludes by offering a final prayer of petition.

Let us confidently place our trust in God as we lay our prayers before the one who always gives us what we need; as we respond, *Lord, let your face shine on us.*

- For patience, perspective, and peace in our work, school, and relationships, we pray, . . . *[all respond]* Lord, let your face shine on us.

- For the hungry and thirsty in body and in spirit, for trust and faith, we pray, . . . *[all respond]* Lord, let your face shine on us.
- For those who are overcome with fear and anxiety, especially for those who suffer from any kind of mental illness, for healing and grace, we pray, . . . *[all respond]* Lord, let your face shine on us.
- For all those who have gone on to their eternal rest in the land of the living, especially *[mention names],* we pray, . . . *[all respond]* Lord, let your face shine on us.
- For the prayers and worries we hold in the silence of our hearts, especially those too painful to speak, we pray, . . . *[all respond]* Lord, let your face shine on us.

God of great abundance,
you know the prayers we speak
and those in the depths of our hearts.
As we place our trust in you,
we know you will always give us what we need.
We make our prayer through Christ Jesus, our Lord.

[All respond.] Amen.

Closing Prayer and Blessing

The following prayer and blessing are led by the presider:

The Lord's Prayer

Gathering our prayers, anxiety, fears, and praise into one, let us offer the prayer Christ himself taught us. *[All join in.]* Our Father . . .

Closing Blessing

Let us bow our heads and pray for God's blessing:
May the Father, who always provides for his children,
bless us and keep us.

[All respond.] Amen.

May Jesus Christ, his Son,
who knows the longings of our hearts,
smile upon us with his grace.

[All respond.] Amen.

And may the Holy Spirit,
the fire of justice and joy in our lives,
grant our hearts peace.

[All respond.] Amen.

In the name of the Father and of the Son and of the Holy Spirit.

[All respond.] Amen.

Sign of Peace

My sisters and brothers, let us go forth sharing with one another a sign of Christ's peace.

In Times of Success and Rejoicing

IN THE CONTEXT OF EVENING PRAYER

Overview

High school students experience many pressures and demands. Yearbooks, service projects, dances, mission trips, sporting events, planning retreats, and academic competitions are significant undertakings for students. They are so significant that they are worthy of celebration upon completion. This prayer service facilitates such thanksgiving. In particular, it celebrates a feeling of victory.

Preparation

Guide for Preparing a Reflection

If you are including a reflection after the Scripture reading, 2 Timothy 4:1–8, give a copy of the following guide to the person who will be leading it and suggest that she or he adapt it to her or his own style and purpose:

> Nothing is sweeter than victory. Late hours, hard work, and pushing yourself further than you thought you could go can be a grueling and stressful experience. But when such sacrifice gives way to reaching another level of excellence, it is all worth it. As a disciple of Jesus Christ, Paul tells Timothy that he has "fought the good fight" (2 Timothy 4:7) and has "finished the race" (verse 7). Paul uses the image of an athlete to describe his dedication to the Lord. The difference between Paul's true victory and the victory of an athlete is a matter of lasting value. If a yearbook has been completed, next year's is just a few months away. If a team has won a championship, it is months away from having to defend the title. Although these successes are sweet, they do not last forever. The lessons learned from hard work and reward are to remind us to work hard for the victory that will last forever—the prize of being united as one family with Jesus as the Lord.

Preparing the Music

When choosing the gathering song for this service, choose something that is familiar to all so that everyone can easily join in singing. The following selections can be found in the second edition of *Gather Comprehensive*, published by GIA Publications:

- "Lift Up Your Hearts," by Roc O'Connor
- "We Praise You," by David Haas
- "Goodness Is Stronger Than Evil," by John Bell
- "Sing Out, Earth and Skies," by Marty Haugen
- "Over My Head" (African American spiritual)

Order of Prayer: In Times of Success and Rejoicing

All the prayers in this service are led by the presider unless otherwise indicated.

Gathering

Once everyone has entered the space, begin with the call to prayer:

> We have gathered this evening to give thanks
> for the success and sense of accomplishment
> we now enjoy.
> Recognizing that God is the source of all things that are good,
> let us stand and begin our prayer.
> *[All make the sign of the cross.]* God, come to my assistance.

[All respond.] Lord, make haste to help me.

> Glory to the Father and to the Son and to the Holy Spirit.

[All respond.] As it was in the beginning, is now and will be forever.

Gathering Song

The presider stands and motions for all to stand. The person leading song invites the assembly to join in singing the gathering song.

At the conclusion of the song, all sit. If necessary, the presider motions for all to sit.

Psalmody

After all are seated, without rushing, the cantor or the choir begins the first psalm. The cantor or the choir sings the verses, and the assembly sings the response. If the psalms are proclaimed, the responses can be used after each verse.

First Psalm: Psalm 141

[All respond.] "Let my prayer rise before you like incense, O Lord, and my hands like an evening off'ring" (*Gather Comprehensive*).

After a brief period of silence following the conclusion of the psalm, the presider stands and motions for all to stand, and he or she proclaims the psalm prayer.

Psalm Prayer

Let us pray. *[Pause.]*
Lord, our God,
the death of your Son, Jesus,
won the ultimate victory for us.
As he gave everything he had as a gift to you,
may our entire lives be pleasing in your sight.
We pray this in the name of Jesus Christ, our Lord.

[All respond.] Amen.

After the psalm prayer, the presider motions for all to sit. Without rushing, the cantor or the choir begins the second psalm.

Second Psalm: Psalm 66

[All respond.] "Let all the earth cry out in joy to the Lord" *(Gather Comprehensive)*.

After a brief period of silence following the conclusion of the psalm, the presider stands and motions for all to stand, and she or he proclaims the psalm prayer.

Psalm Prayer

Let us pray. *[Pause.]*
Almighty God, through our baptism,
we have been given a share in the victory of your Son, Jesus.
Through our baptism, we have been given the gift of the Holy Spirit
to bring us salvation and comfort.
Through our baptism, may we share with the world
the source of our hope and joy.
We ask this through Jesus the Christ.

[All respond.] Amen.

After the psalm prayer, the presider motions for all to sit. Without rushing, the reader or readers stand to proclaim the reading from the Scriptures.

Scripture Reading:
Second Timothy 4:1–8

A reading from the Second Letter of Paul to Timothy:

> In the presence of God and of Christ Jesus, who is to judge the living and the dead, and in view of his appearing and his kingdom, I solemnly urge you: proclaim the message; be persistent whether the time is favorable or unfavorable; convince, rebuke, and encourage, with the utmost patience in teaching. . . .
>
> As for me, I am already being poured out as a libation, and the time of my departure has come. I have fought the good fight, I have finished the race, I have kept the faith. From now on there is reserved for me the crown of righteousness, which the Lord, the righteous judge, will give me on that day, and not only to me but also to all who have longed for his appearing.

The word of the Lord.

[All respond.] Thanks be to God.

Optional Reflection

After the reading, observe a period of silence. If there is to be a reflection, the person giving it stands. If there is no reflection, after the silence, all stand for the canticle.

Canticle

As the cantor begins the canticle, all make the sign of the cross. For evening prayer, the Canticle of Mary is the standard canticle. If the prayer service is held later in the evening, the Canticle of Simeon may be used instead. If the prayer is to be read, see page 119 or 121 for a copy of the text.

Intercessions

All remain standing as the presider invites the assembly to pray the intercessions. After the reader has led the petitions, the presider concludes by offering a final prayer of petition.

> In Christ Jesus, we have won the race and fought the good fight. In confidence that we will reign with him as victors, let us cry out, *Lord, bring us to salvation.*
>
> - For the Church, may it faithfully speak the gospel of freedom, we pray . . . *[all respond]*, Lord, bring us to salvation.
> - For the world, may it be set free from every form of evil, we pray . . . *[all respond]*, Lord, bring us to salvation.
> - For those who labor, may their work benefit themselves and others, we pray . . . *[all respond]*, Lord, bring us to salvation.

- For all of us gathered here, may we acknowledge our accomplishments and be prepared for the work that lies ahead, we pray . . . *[all respond]*, Lord, bring us to salvation.
- For our friends and family, may you return to them the love and support they have given to us, we pray . . . *[all respond]*, Lord, bring us to salvation.

Dear God,
We come to you with hearts overflowing with joy.
We have experienced your help and know it is a sign of your everlasting love for us. Allow us to share our joy with those who are in need of hope.
We ask this through Christ, our Lord.

[All respond.] Amen.

Closing Prayer and Blessing

The following prayer and blessing are led by the presider:

The Lord's Prayer

With happiness that we are members of God's family, let us pray the prayer Jesus, our brother, gave to us. *[All join in.]* Our Father . . .

Closing Blessing

May the Lord bless us,
protect us from everything that is evil,
and bring us to the joy of heaven.
In the name of the Father and of the Son and of the Holy Spirit.

[All respond.] Amen.

Sign of Peace

Let us conclude our prayer with a sign of the peace of Christ.

In Times of Thanks

IN THE CONTEXT OF EVENING PRAYER

Overview

This prayer service is intended to bring together those seeking or celebrating a spirit of gratitude. It may be used during personal, family, or communal times of success or celebration or simply as a reminder that there is *always* something to be grateful for. It is appropriate for various life events, such as births, good grades, college acceptance, and any time prayers have been answered or blessings bestowed. Consider using this service also when the community needs to be reminded of what's right with the world rather than what's wrong. It is also an appropriate service for the celebration of the Thanksgiving holiday. Whatever the situation, the service offers the participants an opportunity to give honor, praise, and glory to the God from whom all blessings come.

Preparation

Guide for Preparing a Reflection

If you are including a reflection after the Scripture reading, Luke 17:11–19, give a copy of the following guide to the person who will be leading it and suggest that she or he adapt it to her or his own style and purpose:

In the Gospel of Luke, we hear an account of the healing of lepers by Jesus. Lepers in first-century Palestine were required by law to live isolated from the community. They were pariahs, relegated to ghettos on the outskirts of cities.

As Luke tells it, one day Jesus is walking with his disciples in the direction of Jerusalem. As they come to a village, they pass by a leper colony. Ten lepers, scaly and deformed, scuttle out, calling to Jesus. They stop at a safe distance and shout to Jesus for mercy. They are hoping for a miracle, and he does not disappoint them.

Jesus tells them to go see the priest, which is necessary before they can return to the community. On their way to the priest, they suddenly discover their leprosy is gone! But only one of the healed lepers returns to Jesus to thank him. He throws himself on the ground before Jesus in gratefulness. He is the only one who knows and appreciates the value of what he has been given.

It sometimes takes a healed Samaritan leper in ancient Palestine to see clearly the importance of gratefulness. It takes someone who is keenly and daily aware of the joy of having made it through adversity, to be able to break forth in gratitude. Such a person practices *thanksgiving as a way of life*.

If we do nothing else on this earth, let us at least be grateful. Let us be thankful in the morning, thankful at noon, thankful at night, thankful all day long. Let us make thanksgiving a way of life—our way of life.

Preparing the Music

When choosing the gathering song for this service, choose something that is familiar to all so that everyone can easily join in singing. The following selections can be found in the second edition of *Gather Comprehensive,* published by GIA Publications:

- "In the Lord I'll Be Ever Thankful," by Taizé
- "We Give You Thanks," by David Haas
- "Let All Things Now Living" (traditional)
- "Sing of the Lord's Goodness," by Ernest Sands

Order of Prayer: In Times of Thanks

All the prayers in this service are led by the presider unless otherwise indicated.

Gathering Song

The person leading song stands, motions for all to stand, and invites the assembly to join in singing the gathering song.

At the conclusion of the song, all sit. If necessary, the presider motions for all to sit.

Psalmody

After all are seated, without rushing, the cantor or the choir begins the first psalm. The cantor or the choir sings the verses, and the assembly sings the response. If the psalms are proclaimed, the responses can be used after each verse.

First Psalm: Psalm 141

[All respond.] "Let my prayer rise before you like incense, O Lord, and my hands like an evening off'ring" *(Gather Comprehensive)*.

After a brief period of silence following the conclusion of the psalm, the presider stands and motions for all to stand, and he or she proclaims the psalm prayer.

Psalm Prayer

> Let us pray. *[Pause.]*
> From uplifted hearts full of gratitude,
> may our prayers of thanksgiving rise to you,
> God of all gifts and great generosity.
> We are thankful for times of stillness that allow us to
> experience the presence of your Holy Spirit within,
> the Spirit who prays continuously.
> In our times of prayer, heal us within and without.
> Replenish our spirits with new strength
> and prepare us to meet each day with renewed thankfulness and joy.
> May we in prayerful communion with you

allow our lives to reveal your goodness and glory.
We ask this through Christ, our Lord.

[All respond.] Amen.

After all are seated, without rushing, the cantor or the choir begins the second psalm.

Second Psalm: Psalm 66

[All respond.] "Let all the earth cry out in joy to the Lord" *(Gather Comprehensive).*

After a brief period of silence following the psalm, the presider stands and motions for all to stand, and she or he proclaims the psalm prayer.

Psalm Prayer

Let us pray. *[Pause.]*
God of all of that is good,
how great are your deeds for us.
We sing of our love for you,
joining our voices with choirs of angels
and with all the faithful of every time and place.
This evening, and always,
we cry out in joy to the glory of your name.
Most gracious and awesome God,
we lift up our spirits in gratitude
for all you have done for us.
Blessed be your name, now and always.

[All respond.] Amen.

After the psalm prayer, the presider motions for all to sit. Without rushing, the reader or readers stand to proclaim the reading from the Scriptures.

Scripture Reading: Luke 17:11–19

A reading from the holy Gospel according to Luke:

On the way to Jerusalem Jesus was going through the region between Samaria and Galilee. As he entered a village, ten lepers approached him. Keeping their distance, they called out, saying, "Jesus, Master, have mercy on us!" When he saw them, he said to them, "Go and show yourselves to the priests." And as they went, they were made clean. Then one of them, when he saw that he was healed, turned back, praising God with a loud voice. He prostrated himself at Jesus' feet and thanked him. And he was a Samaritan. Then Jesus asked, "Were not ten made clean? But the other nine, where are they?

57

Was none of them found to return and give praise to God except this foreigner?" Then he said to him, "Get up and go on your way; your faith has made you well."

The word of the Lord.

[All respond.] Thanks be to God.

Optional Reflection

After the reading, observe a period of silence. If there is to be a reflection, the person giving it stands. If there is no reflection, after the silence, all stand for the canticle.

Canticle

As the cantor begins the canticle, all make the sign of the cross. For evening prayer, the Canticle of Mary is the standard canticle. If the prayer service is held later in the evening, the Canticle of Simeon may be used instead. If the prayer is to be read, see page 119 or 121 for a copy of the text.

Intercessions

All remain standing as the presider invites the assembly to pray the intercessions. After the reader has led the petitions, the presider concludes by offering a final prayer of petition.

Let us offer our prayers to our ever-generous God, as we say, *God of goodness, we offer this prayer.*

- We pray that we might always appreciate the beauty and wonder of creation, we pray . . . *[all respond]*, God of goodness, we offer this prayer.
- For our daily food, for our homes and families and friends, we pray . . . *[all respond]*, God of goodness, we offer this prayer.
- We pray for health, strength, and skill to work, and for leisure to rest and play, we pray . . . *[all respond]*, God of goodness, we offer this prayer.
- We pray for those who are brave and courageous, patient in suffering, and faithful in adversity, we pray . . . *[all respond]*, God of goodness, we offer this prayer.
- For all who pursue peace, justice, and truth, we pray . . . *[all respond]*, God of goodness, we offer this prayer.
- Today, we give thanks especially for . . . *[allow time for verbal response from the assembly]*. And so, we pray . . . *[all respond]*, God of goodness, we offer this prayer.

Loving God, we offer all that we have
and all that we are to you.
May our prayers be received as incense before you.

May all our words and actions give you praise and glory,
now and always, we pray.

[All respond.] Amen.

Closing Prayer and Blessing

The following prayer and blessing are led by the presider:

The Lord's Prayer

And as we remember the gift of your goodness, O Lord, we pray the prayer that your Son taught us. *[All join in.]* Our Father . . .

Closing Blessing

Let us bow our heads and pray for God's blessing:
Accept, O Lord, our thanks and praise for all that you have done for us.
We thank you for the splendor of the whole creation,
for the beauty of this world,
for the wonder of life,
and for the mystery of love.

[All respond.] Amen.

We thank you for the blessing of family and friends,
and for the loving care that surrounds us on every side.
We thank you for setting us at tasks that demand our best efforts
and for leading us to accomplishments that satisfy and delight us.

[All respond.] Amen.

Above all, we thank you for your Son, Jesus Christ,
for the truth of his word and the example of his life.
Grant us the gift of your Spirit, and through your Spirit,
at all times and in all places,
may we give thanks to you in all things.

[All respond.] Amen.

And may God bless us, Father, Son, and Spirit.

[All respond.] Amen.

Sign of Peace

My brothers and sisters, let us joyfully give one another the sign of fellowship and peace.

When Healing and Forgiveness Are Needed

IN THE CONTEXT OF EVENING PRAYER

Overview

Sin and pain are part of human living. All sin is communal, but at times it impacts a community in a particularly poignant way. Young people are generally loyal to their friends. When two friends fight, an entire group can feel forced to take sides. What is needed is reconciliation. This prayer service is ideal for Ash Wednesday, for other days during the Lenten season, and for preparation for celebrating the sacrament of Penance and Reconciliation. However, if the relationships among the members of a youth group are discordant, this service might serve as a way for the young people to reconcile with one another.

Preparation

Guide for Preparing a Reflection

If you are including a reflection after the Scripture reading, 2 Corinthians 2:5–11, give a copy of the following guide to the person who will be leading it and suggest that he or she adapt it to his or her own style and purpose:

Among the Christians in Corinth, somebody sinned—badly. Pain was inflicted upon the whole community because of this person's wrongdoing. We don't know what it was, but we know it wasn't pretty. But Paul urges the church not to overburden the person.

If someone has sinned against us, we want the person to pay. We give the cold shoulder. We talk behind her or his back and try to get others as mad at that person as we are. We try to bring the person down.

If we have sinned against others, we can feel as though we'll never be accepted again. We can feel very ashamed of ourselves and think that God is angry with us.

Paul urges the Corinthians to outwit Satan. If we have been wronged, outwit Satan by forgiving. If we have been the sinner, outwit Satan by accepting God's gracious and abundant forgiveness. Also, believe it when people tell you that you are forgiven.

Preparing the Music

When choosing the gathering song for this service, choose something that is familiar to all so that everyone can easily join in singing. The following selections can be found in the second edition of *Gather Comprehensive,* published by GIA Publications:

- **"Change Our Hearts,"** by Rory Cooney
- "Jesus, Heal Us," by David Haas
- "Healer of Our Every Ill," by Marty Haugen
- "Precious Lord, Take My Hand" (traditional African American)
- **"Hands of Healing,"** by Marty Haugen

Additional Considerations

As a prayer where healing and forgiveness is being sought, it would be valuable to include some of the images of repentance the Church provides:

- purple altar clothes
- ashes
- a large cross

Whether or not this service is prayed in the Lenten season, it can recall the images of the season as symbols. Also, using such symbols can help the group better participate in Lent when the season does indeed occur.

Order of Prayer: When Healing and Forgiveness Are Needed

All the prayers in this service are led by the presider unless otherwise indicated.

Gathering

The presider stands and motions for all to stand. The presider says:

> This evening we are gathered together and are reminded that we are fallen.
> We are sinful.
> Yet, we are loved beyond imagine.
> Let us open ourselves to receiving the immense love of God as we pray.
> *[All make the sign of the cross.]* God, come to my assistance.

[All respond.] Lord, make haste to help me.

> Glory to the Father and to the Son and to the Holy Spirit.

[All respond.] As it was in the beginning, is now and will be forever.

Gathering Song

The presider stands and motions for all to stand and join in singing the gathering song.

At the conclusion of the song, all sit. If necessary, the presider motions for all to sit.

Psalmody

After all are seated, without rushing, the cantor or the choir begins the first psalm. The cantor or the choir sings the verses, and the assembly sings the response. If the psalms are proclaimed, the responses can be used after each verse.

First Psalm: Psalm 51

[All respond.] "Be merciful, O Lord, we have sinned" *(Gather Comprehensive).*

After a brief period of silence following the conclusion of the psalm, the presider stands and motions for all to stand, and she or he proclaims the psalm prayer.

Psalm Prayer

> Let us pray. *[Pause.]*
> Father, you intend for us to enjoy your friendship.
> Because of your desire to keep us close to you,
> you sent your Son, Jesus.
> Dear God, look inside our hearts
> and see that we truly want to follow the right path
> and that we are sorry for the wrong things we have done.
> Heal us.
> Forgive us.
> Renew us.
> Join us ever more closely with the people we love
> and with your Son, Jesus, in whose name we pray.

[All respond.] Amen.

After the psalm prayer, the presider motions for all to sit. Without rushing, the cantor or the choir begins the second psalm.

Second Psalm: Psalm 121

[All respond.] "Our help comes from the Lord, the maker of heaven and earth" *(Gather Comprehensive).*

After a brief period of silence following the conclusion of the psalm, the presider stands and motions for all to stand, and he or she proclaims the psalm prayer.

Psalm Prayer

> Let us pray. *[Pause.]*
> Lord God, when we seek your forgiveness,
> your heart leaps with joy.
> Let us feel the healing rays of your forgiveness.
> May we not be burdened by guilt.

Rather, may we have confidence in your love,
and may we offer to you a sacrifice of praise.
May our songs, words, and deeds
be an offering of praise to you.
We ask this through Christ Jesus.

[All respond.] Amen.

After the psalm prayer, the presider motions for all to sit. Without rushing, the reader or readers stand to proclaim the reading from the Scriptures.

Scripture Reading:

Second Corinthians 2:5–11

A reading from the Second Letter of Paul to the Corinthians:

But if anyone has caused pain, he has caused it not to me, but to some extent—not to exaggerate it—to all of you. This punishment by the majority is enough for such a person; so now instead you should forgive and console him, so that he may not be overwhelmed by excessive sorrow. So I urge you to reaffirm your love for him. I wrote for this reason: to test you and to know whether you are obedient in everything. Anyone whom you forgive, I also forgive. What I have forgiven, if I have forgiven anything, has been for your sake in the presence of Christ. And we do this so that we may not be outwitted by Satan; for we are not ignorant of his designs.

The word of the Lord.

[All respond.] Thanks be to God.

Optional Reflection

After the reading, observe a period of silence. If there is to be a reflection, the person giving it stands. If there is no reflection, after the silence, all stand for the canticle.

Canticle

As the cantor begins the canticle, all make the sign of the cross. For evening prayer, the Canticle of Mary is the standard canticle. If the prayer service is held later in the evening, the Canticle of Simeon may be used instead. If the prayer is to be read, see page 119 or 121 for a copy of the text.

Intercessions

All remain standing as the presider invites the assembly to pray the intercessions. After the reader has led the petitions, the presider concludes by offering a final prayer of petition.

The Lord Jesus has taken on our humanity and understands our weakness. Let us call out to Jesus, the one who has been tested in every way but never sinned, saying, *We praise you for your mercy.*

- Lord Jesus, you came to unite the whole world together in you. Heal all that divides us. We pray . . . *[all respond]*, We praise you for your mercy.
- Lord Jesus, you gave the Church the mission of reconciling everyone to you. May the Church never stop laboring for reconciliation. We pray . . . *[all respond]*, We praise you for your mercy.
- Lord Jesus, we remember world leaders and the power they possess. May they be people who work for justice and solidarity. We pray . . . *[all respond]*, We praise you for your mercy.
- Lord Jesus, we pray for those who are blinded by sin. May your Holy Spirit change their hearts into love. We pray . . . *[all respond]*, We praise you for your mercy.
- Lord Jesus, we pray for ourselves. When others wrong us, help us to forgive. When others forgive us, help us to receive their forgiveness. We pray . . . *[all respond]*, We praise you for your mercy.
- Lord Jesus, we give our families to you. We ask that our homes may be places where your peace and harmony reign. We pray . . . *[all respond]*, We praise you for your mercy.
- Lord Jesus, we pray for our friends. We ask that our relationships draw us closer to you and not further away from you. We pray . . . *[all respond]*, We praise you for your mercy.

All merciful God,
throughout all of time the people you chose
have disobeyed your commands.
Help us to be faithful.
Give us your grace to overcome our selfishness.
Mold us into people who always give your light to others.
We ask this through Jesus the Lord.

[All respond.] Amen.

Closing Prayer and Blessing

The following prayer and blessing are led by the presider:

The Lord's Prayer

Asking God to forgive us as we forgive others, let us seek God's
Reign as we pray. *[All join in.]* Our Father . . .

Closing Blessing

God of mercy and forgiveness,
we thank you for the healing presence of your Holy Spirit.
You have taken away our guilt and replaced it with joy.
You have taken away our shame and replaced it with confidence.
May we always live in the light of your truth.
We ask this through Christ the Lord.

[All respond.] Amen.

May the Lord bless us,
protect us from everything that is evil,
and bring us to the joy of heaven.
In the name of the Father and of the Son and of the Holy Spirit.

[All respond.] Amen.

Sign of Peace

Let us conclude our prayer by extending to one another a sign of
God's peace.

When Hope Is Needed

IN THE CONTEXT OF MORNING PRAYER

Overview

This prayer service is intended to bring hope during times of despair, consolation in times of suffering, and light in times of darkness. It may be used during difficult personal, family, or communal times. It is appropriate for various life events, such as unexpected tragedies and uncertain times in the life of a young person (waiting for college acceptance, difficulties with school work, and so forth). Whatever the situation, this service offers the participants an opportunity to pray about and work toward a greater sense of hope in unforeseen circumstances.

Preparation

Guide for Preparing a Reflection

If you are including a reflection after the Scripture reading, Job 1:13–21, give a copy of the following guide to the person who will be leading it and suggest that he or she adapt it to his or her own style and purpose:

> We learn at the start of the Book of Job that Job has vast land holdings: thousands of sheep; hundreds of oxen, camels, and donkeys; many servants; and ten children, including seven sons, the clearest sign of wealth in that ancient culture. But it all collapses in short order, and Job is left in misery and grief, suddenly a man of sorrow and suffering.
>
> Job simply cannot understand why a blameless and upright man such as himself, whose loyalty to God is profound, should suffer a series of calamities in his life. Anyone who has been dealt what feels like a capricious and serious blow in life can sympathize with Job. None of it is deserved.
>
> At times we feel as if we are abandoned, alone, and about to be overwhelmed by life. Then all of a sudden God comes to us through the comforting words of a stranger, a phone call from a friend, the squeeze of a hand, a gentle touch by a loved one, or an inner strength that comes from somewhere deep inside. In the face of the trials and tragedies of life, we discover in all sorts of ways that God is with us! This is the Good News, and the Good News brings hope to us and to the crazy, hurting world we live in. Many of us have experienced terrible things, and all of us have experienced pain and hurt. So what do we do? How do we cope? How do we find hope in the face of it all? Well, for one thing, we face the reality that terrible things do

happen. And then, like Job, we hold on to the heart of our faith. We hold on to the knowledge that God is with us in the midst of it all, actively working to bring hope and healing to our lives.

Preparing the Music

When choosing the gathering song for this service, choose something that is familiar to all so that everyone can easily join in singing. The following selections can be found in the second edition of *Gather Comprehensive*, published by GIA Publications:

- "Lord of All Hopefulness" (traditional Gaelic)
- "How Can I Keep from Singing?" (traditional Quaker hymn)
- "Christ Be Our Light," by Bernadette Farrell
- "Over My Head" (African American spiritual)
- "All Will Be Well," by Steve Warner

Order of Prayer: When Hope Is Needed

All the prayers in this service are led by the presider unless otherwise indicated.

Gathering

The presider stands and motions for all to stand. The presider says:

> Blessed be God eternal, watching over all we do.
> Blessed be Jesus, our wisdom, companion in the striving.
> Blessed be the divine Spirit, constantly renewing our spirit of hope.

[All respond.] Amen.

Gathering Song

The presider motions for all to join in singing the gathering song.

At the conclusion of the song, all sit. If necessary, the presider motions for all to sit.

Psalmody

After all are seated, without rushing, the cantor or the choir begins the first psalm. The cantor or the choir sings the verses, and the assembly sings the response. If the psalms are proclaimed, the responses can be used after each verse.

First Psalm: Psalm 63

[All respond.] "As morning breaks I look to you; I look to you, O Lord, to be my strength this day" *(Gather Comprehensive)*.

After a brief period of silence following the conclusion of the psalm, the presider stands and motions for all to stand, and she or he proclaims the psalm prayer.

Psalm Prayer

Let us pray. *[Pause.]*
Good and gracious God,
As morning breaks,
we look to you to be our strength this day.
Breathe into us the Spirit who dwells in all hearts.
Open our eyes to see your kindness.
Open our ears to cherish your word of hope.
Open our lips to speak your praise.
Open our hands to receive the grace only you can provide us.
In our times of trials and doubt, help us to cling and hold fast to you.
This morning, and all mornings, keep us singing of your goodness
   and glory.
We ask this through Christ, our Lord.

[All respond.] Amen.

After the psalm prayer, the presider motions for all to sit. Without rushing, the cantor or the choir begins the second psalm.

Second Psalm: Psalm 138

[All respond.] "Lord, on the day that I cried out for help, you answered me" *(Gather Comprehensive).*

After a brief period of silence following the conclusion of the psalm, the presider stands and motions for all to stand, and he or she proclaims the psalm prayer.

Psalm Prayer

Let us pray. *[Pause.]*
Gracious God, tireless guardian of your people,
ever prepared to hear the cries of your chosen ones,
teach us to rely, day and night, on your care.
On you we call, Lord God,
in all places and through all circumstances,
to give strength to our souls.
We praise you for your faithfulness and love,
and we thank you for the guidance and hope you offer us.
Be with us today, God from whom all encouragement comes,
support our prayer, so that we may not grow weary.
Impel us to seek your enduring and ever-present help always.
We ask this through Christ, our Lord.

[All respond.] Amen.

After the psalm prayer, the presider motions for all to sit. Without rushing, the reader or readers stand to proclaim the reading from the Scriptures.

Scripture Reading:
Job 1:13–21

A reading from the Book of Job:

One day when his sons and daughters were eating and drinking wine in the eldest brother's house, a messenger came to Job and said, "The oxen were plowing and the donkeys feeding beside them, and the Sabeans fell on them and carried them off, and killed the servants with the edge of the sword; I alone have escaped to tell you." While he was still speaking, another came and said, "The fire of God fell from heaven and burned up the sheep and the servants, and consumed them; I alone have escaped to tell you." While he was still speaking, another came and said, "The Chaldeans formed three columns, made a raid on the camels and carried them off, and killed the servants with the edge of the sword; I alone have escaped to tell you." While he was still speaking, another came and said, "Your sons and daughters were eating and drinking wine in their eldest brother's house, and suddenly a great wind came across the desert, struck the four corners of the house, and it fell on the young people, and they are dead; I alone have escaped to tell you."

Then Job arose, tore his robe, shaved his head, and fell on the ground and worshiped. He said, "Naked I came from my mother's womb, and naked shall I return there; the Lord gave, and the Lord has taken away; blessed be the name of the Lord."

The word of the Lord.

[All respond.] Thanks be to God.

Optional Reflection

After the reading, observe a period of silence. If there is to be a reflection, the person giving it stands. If there is no reflection, after the silence, all stand for the canticle.

Canticle

As the cantor begins the Canticle of Zechariah (the Benedictus), the presider and all make the sign of the cross. If this is to be read, see page 120 for a copy of the text.

Intercessions

All remain standing as the presider invites the assembly to pray the intercessions. After the reader has led the petitions, the presider concludes by offering a final prayer of petition.

All-powerful God, you dwell within us during our times of weakness and strength, and so we bring to you the prayers that dwell within us, as we say, *Spirit of hope, come sustain us.*

- In the fear and apprehension, hesitation, and uncertainty that we experience, we pray . . . *[all respond]*, Spirit of hope, come sustain us.
- In the sense of mystery of the unknown, and in the wonder that dawns in us, as we seek to follow you, we pray . . . *[all respond]*, Spirit of hope, come sustain us.
- In the pain and restlessness that we sometimes experience, we pray . . . *[all respond]*, Spirit of hope, come sustain us.
- For all who grow tired and weary, when burdens make us falter and we want to stop, we pray . . . *[all respond]*, Spirit of hope, come sustain us.
- When we grow in insight, as your wisdom prompts us when to let go and when to take up, we pray . . . *[all respond]*, Spirit of hope, come sustain us.
- When we glimpse your presence and excite in the sense of your closeness, we pray . . . *[all respond]*, Spirit of hope, come sustain us.

We thank you, Lord, our God, for these moments of prayer.
Grant us your consolation in the midst
of the difficult moments we are passing through,
and lead us to eternal life.
We ask this through your Son, our Lord, Jesus Christ,

[All respond.] Amen.

Closing Prayer and Blessing

The following prayer and blessing are led by the presider:

The Lord's Prayer

O God of hope and new life,
help us to celebrate the joy of abundant life
as you intend for us.
Through your great love,
let all who need you, especially now,

feel your presence and know your peace,
as shown through your Son, Jesus Christ,
who also taught us how to pray. *[All join in.]* Our Father . . .

Closing Blessing

Let us bow our heads and pray for God's blessing:
May the God of new beginnings
lead us forward this day.

[All respond.] Amen.

May the God who brings us new life in Christ
fill us with resurrection and joy this day.

[All respond.] Amen.

May the God who abides within us
be revealed to all we meet this day.

[All respond.] Amen.

May the God who consoles and protects us
soothe any heartache this day.

[All respond.] Amen.

May the God who desires abundance of life for all creation
renew our spirits this day.

[All respond.] Amen.

And may God bless us, Father, Son, and Spirit.

[All respond.] Amen.

Sign of Peace

Let us conclude our prayer with a sign of the peace of Christ.

In Times of Transition

IN THE CONTEXT OF EVENING PRAYER

Overview

The lives of young people change rather rapidly. They seem to be in a constant state of transition. Whether they are moving into high school or moving into college, young people are always opening a new chapter in their lives. These can be frightening times. But they can also be very exciting times as well. This service is appropriate for times of change when the future is both scary and exciting.

Preparation

Guide for Preparing a Reflection

If you are including a reflection after the Scripture reading, 1 Corinthians 2:7–11, give a copy of the following guide to the person who will be leading it and suggest that she or he adapt it to her or his own style and purpose:

> What is in store for you? God only knows. Will you fail or will you succeed? Will you be happy or will you be miserable? God only knows. This is a transition time for you. You are saying good-bye to the familiar, and you are being asked to embrace something new. It is exciting, but it is also scary. A wise person once said, "We don't know the future. But we

know someone who does." The future, your future, belongs to God.

> In the reading from First Corinthians, we hear that God has something spectacular in store for those who love God. We cannot begin to imagine the wonderful things God has prepared for us. It is so far beyond our comprehension that only the Holy Spirit knows. Will you hate the change? It is quite possible that you might. It is difficult to feel as if you are not in control of your life. However, it is during these times of transition that you need to place your trust in God's love and care for you. Despite any event that looks like a mistake, God has the ability to bring good out of it.

Preparing the Music

When choosing the gathering song for this service, choose something that is familiar to all so everyone can easily join in singing. The following selections can be found in the second edition of *Gather Comprehensive*, published by GIA Publications:
- "Canticle of the Turning," by Rory Cooney
- "Open My Eyes," by Jesse Manibusan
- "Covenant Hymn," by Rory Cooney and Gary Daigle
- "We Walk by Faith," by Marty Haugen
- "Lead Me Guide, Guide Me," by Doris M. Akers

Order of Prayer: In Times of Transition

All the prayers in this service are led by the presider unless otherwise indicated.

Gathering

The presider stands and motions for all to stand. The presider says:

> We have gathered here this evening
> to place our future into God's hands.
> As we pray, let us remember that God has called each of us
> by name and intends to give us a future full of hope.
> Holding on to this in faith, let us begin our prayer.
> *[All make the sign of the cross.]* God, come to my assistance.

[All respond.] Lord, make haste to help me.

> Glory to the Father and to the Son and to the Holy Spirit.

[All respond.] As it was in the beginning, is now and will be forever.

Gathering Song

The presider motions for all to join in singing the gathering song.

At the conclusion of the song, all sit. If necessary, the presider motions for all to sit.

Psalmody

After all are seated, without rushing, the cantor or the choir begins the first psalm. The cantor or the choir sings the verses, and the assembly sings the response. If the psalms are proclaimed, the responses can be used after each verse.

First Psalm: Psalm 141

[All respond.] "Let my prayer rise before you like incense, O Lord, and my hands like an evening off'ring" *(Gather Comprehensive)*.

After a brief period of silence following the conclusion of the psalm, the presider stands and motions for all to stand, and he or she proclaims the psalm prayer.

Psalm Prayer

Let us pray. *[Pause.]*
We call upon you, God,
during this time of excitement and uncertainty.
Just as incense rises before you,
we also lift our hands.
Empty-handed we come into your presence
acknowledging that our lives are in your hands, not ours.
We joyfully give ourselves to you in praise,
and with joy we look to our future.
We pray this prayer in the name of Jesus Christ, our Lord.

[All respond.] Amen.

After the psalm prayer, the presider motions for all to sit. Without rushing, the cantor or the choir begins the second psalm.

Second Psalm: Psalm 40

[All respond.] "Here I am, Lord, here I am. I come to do your will" *(Gather Comprehensive).*

After a brief period of silence following the conclusion of the psalm, the presider stands and motions for all to stand, and she or he proclaims the psalm prayer.

Psalm Prayer

Let us pray. *[Pause.]*
Lord, when we are uncertain about the future,
you ask us to trust.
When we are waiting for your help,
you ask us to be patient.
When we cry out,
you tell us that you listen.
Lord, you work wonders to prove your love for us.
You guide us through our future
and take us to places beyond our imagination.
May your faithful give us hope during times of uncertainty.
We ask this through Christ, our Lord.

[All respond.] Amen.

After the psalm prayer, the presider motions for all to sit. Without rushing, the reader or readers stand to proclaim the reading from the Scriptures.

Scripture Reading:
First Corinthians 2:7–11

A reading from the First Letter of Paul to the Corinthians:

But we speak God's wisdom, secret and hidden, which God decreed before the ages for our glory. None of the rulers of this age understood this; for if they had, they would not have crucified the Lord of glory. But, as it is written,

"What no eye has seen, nor ear heard,
nor the human heart conceived,
what God has prepared for those who love him"—

these things God has revealed to us through the Spirit; for the Spirit searches everything, even the depths of God. For what human being knows what is truly human except the human spirit that is within? So also no one comprehends what is truly God's except the Spirit of God.

The word of the Lord.

[All respond.] Thanks be to God.

Optional Reflection

After the reading, observe a period of silence. If there is to be a reflection, the person giving it stands. If there is no reflection, after the silence, all stand for the canticle.

Canticle

As the cantor begins the canticle, all make the sign of the cross. For evening prayer, the Canticle of Mary is the standard canticle. If the prayer service is held later in the evening, the Canticle of Simeon may be used instead. If the prayer is to be read, see page 119 or 121 for a copy of the text.

Intercessions

All remain standing as the presider invites the assembly to pray the intercessions. After the reader has led the petitions, the presider concludes by offering a final prayer of petition.

Lord, at every turn in our lives, you are there asking if we love with all that we are. We say yes, Lord, and offer ourselves to you as we pray, *Lord, we are your servants.*

- Lord, for the future of the Church, may the Church constantly draw people into a deeper relationship with your Son, Jesus, we pray . . . *[all respond],* Lord, we are your servants.
- Lord for the future of the world, we ask that all those without hope for a better future be given the comfort of your Holy Spirit, we pray . . . *[all respond],* Lord, we are your servants.
- For all who do not have the freedom to pursue their own future, we ask, dear Christ, that you liberate them from their oppression, we pray . . . *[all respond],* Lord, we are your servants.

- For our friends and family who join us on our road, we ask that they may be able to accept any changes that happen along our path, we pray . . . *[all respond]*, Lord, we are your servants.
- For ourselves as we look toward a new place in our lives, may we always place you, our God, at the center of our lives, we pray . . . *[all respond]*, Lord, we are your servants.

God, you are the alpha and the omega.
You are the beginning and the end.
With trust in your everlasting care,
we present these prayers to you in confidence
through Jesus, your Son and our Lord.

Closing Prayer and Blessing

The following prayer and blessing are led by the presider:

The Lord's Prayer

Looking at a new time in our lives, it can be difficult to find the right words or to know how to pray, so hear us, O God, as we pray with the words your Son has given to us. *[All join in.]* Our Father . . .

Closing Blessing

Lord, our God,
you ask us to preach and to live the Gospel of your Son, Jesus,
in season and out of season,
in good times and in difficult times.
As we move forward from here,
help us to keep you first and to share with everyone we meet
the Good News of your Son, Jesus.

[All respond.] Amen.

May the Lord bless us,
protect us from everything that is evil,
and bring us to the joy of heaven.
In the name of the Father and of the Son and of the Holy Spirit.

[All respond.] Amen.

Sign of Peace

Let us conclude our prayer with a sign of the peace of Christ.

Order of Prayer: In Times of Transition: Permission to reproduce for program use is granted. © 2004 by Saint Mary's Press.

In Times of Mission

IN THE CONTEXT OF MORNING PRAYER

Overview

This prayer service is intended for times of mission, that is, times when young people (and older ones too) are called forth to serve one another and those outside the Church community. It may be used at the start of a service project or mission trip or any time when the congregation is responding to the needs of the Church and the community. Whatever the situation, this service offers participants an opportunity to reflect on God's calling in their lives and to pray for their own (and others') response to such a call.

Preparation

Guide for Preparing a Reflection

If you are including a reflection after the Scripture reading, Luke 17:5–10, give a copy of the following guide to the person who will be leading it and suggest that he or she adapt it to his or her own style and purpose:

> In the Gospel reading, we hear the disciples cry out to Jesus, a cry that perhaps you have made at one time or another. They felt, as ones who wanted to follow Jesus, that what they faced was too much for them. It was too much

for their small faith to handle, and so they cry out to God. When the disciples said to Jesus, "Increase our faith" (Luke 17:5), they had heard more than they thought their hearts could bear. Jesus had talked a lot about the coming Kingdom and what they were supposed to do about it, how they were to serve it, and what the future was going to look like. It overwhelmed them. They didn't feel up to it. They thought they weren't ready or able to do what Jesus was asking of them. And so they say to Jesus: "Well if it's going to be like that, you had better give us some more faith . . . please! Now! Right away. We are going to need it."

In this parable, Jesus points out to us that he has already given us all that it takes to get the work done. Too many of us look at ourselves instead of God. We look at ourselves and we say—I can't do it. I am not strong enough, wise enough, loving enough, giving enough. I do not have the money, the power, or the faith to succeed at what I am being asked to do. And that is completely true—we are not able! But God is able, and when we take hold of God and believe, God's power is able to flow through us—and God works through us. The good news is that we are not alone, that God cares, that God works in the lives of those who believe, that all we need to do is reach down to that little seed within us and begin to do what it is that we have been called to do, and God will do the rest. There will be no mulberry tree planted in the ocean. But there will be a Lord who watches over us and calls us God's own.

Preparing the Music

When choosing the gathering song for this service, choose something that is familiar to all so that everyone can easily join in singing. The following selections can be found in the second edition of *Gather Comprehensive,* published by GIA Publications:

- "Here Am I," by Dan Damon
- "Take, O Take Me As I Am," by John Bell
- "What You Have Done for Me," by Tony Alonso
- "We Are Called," by David Haas
- "The Summons," by John Bell

Additional Considerations

Consider placing a basket filled with small packages of mustard seeds on a small table at the entrance of the prayer space. At the conclusion of the service, invite the participants to take home a package as a reminder of what it is that God has called them to do.

Order of Prayer: In Times of Mission

All the prayers in this service are led by the presider unless otherwise indicated.

Gathering Song

The person leading song stands, motions for all to stand, and invites the assembly to join in singing the gathering song.

At the conclusion of the song, all sit. If necessary, the presider motions for all to sit.

Psalmody

After all are seated, without rushing, the cantor or the choir begins the psalm. The cantor or the choir sings the verses and the assembly sings the response. If the psalms are proclaimed, the response can be used after each verse.

First Psalm: Psalm 63

[*All respond.*] "As morning breaks I look to you; I look to you, O Lord, to be my strength this day" (*Gather Comprehensive*).

After a brief period of silence following the conclusion of the psalm, the presider stands and motions for all to stand, and she or he proclaims the psalm prayer.

Psalm Prayer

Let us pray. [*Pause.*]
As morning breaks we look upon you, O God,
to be our strength, to be our guide, to be our help this day.
Help us to follow close behind you
knowing that your strong right hand holds us securely.
Gentle protector, strong deliverer,
in the night you are our confidence:
from first light we ask that you be our joy.
With all your sons and daughters of faith,
in all times and places,
we will praise and bless you as long as we live.

[*All respond.*] Amen.

After the psalm prayer, the presider motions for all to sit. Without rushing, the cantor or the choir begins the second psalm.

Second Psalm: Psalm 40

[All respond.] "Here I am Lord, here I am. I come to do your will" *(Gather Comprehensive).*

After a brief period of silence following the conclusion of the psalm, the presider stands and motions for all to stand, and he or she proclaims the psalm prayer.

Psalm Prayer

> Let us pray. *[Pause.]*
> Eternal God,
> We come before you this morning in recognition of your calling,
> your invitation to us to share
> in your creative and healing work.
> Help us to listen for your call,
> help us to be able to recognize it and to accept it.
> Help us discover your word and your will for our lives.
> God of all our moments, of our days and our nights,
> you speak and you act in the world around us,
> not only to call all people to you but also to
> direct and guide us in faithfulness and truth.
> Awaken us this morning, O Lord,
> to hear what you would say to us.
> Help us to open our ears, our eyes,
> and our hearts to your presence.
> Help us to know when it is your voice we are hearing.
> We ask this through Christ, our Lord.

[All respond.] Amen.

After the psalm prayer, the presider motions for all to sit. Without rushing, the reader or readers stand to proclaim the reading from the Scriptures.

Scripture Reading: Luke 17:5–10

A reading from the holy Gospel according to Luke:

> The apostles said to the Lord, "Increase our faith!" The Lord replied, "If you had faith the size of a mustard seed, you could say to this mulberry tree, 'Be uprooted and planted in the sea,' and it would obey you.

"Who among you would say to your slave who has just come in from plowing or tending sheep in the field, 'Come here at once and take your place at the table'? Would you not rather say to him, 'Prepare supper for me, put on your apron and serve me while I eat and drink; later you may eat and drink'? Do you thank the slave for doing what was commanded? So you also, when you have done all that you were ordered to do, say, 'We are worthless slaves; we have done only what we ought to have done!'"

The word of the Lord.

[All respond.] Thanks be to God.

Optional Reflection

After the reading, observe a period of silence. If there is to be a reflection, the person giving it stands. If there is no reflection, after the silence, all stand for the canticle.

Canticle

As the cantor begins the Canticle of Zechariah (the Benedictus), the presider and all make the sign of the cross. If this is to be read, see page 120 for a copy of the text.

Intercessions

All remain standing as the presider invites the assembly to pray the intercessions. After the reader has led the petitions, the presider concludes by offering a final prayer of petition.

Let us pray, saying, *God of faithfulness, hear our prayer.*

- Welcoming God, we pray for the Church, that it might be a house of welcome for all people. Move in us so that we might indeed stand upon the promises you have made to us and help us to use the faith we already have to do that which you will for us. For this we pray . . . *[all respond]*, God of faithfulness, hear our prayer.
- Lord, we consider today your Church around the world, we pray for all the people we meet in this church and in your Church beyond these doors. We pray for those who teach and those who sing, for those who look like us and those who are different, for those who are young and those who are old. We praise you for the diversity we have—the uniqueness that each member of your body brings to the whole. We ask that you might help us always to be understanding and loving toward all who call upon your name— and also toward those who do not. For these things we pray . . . *[all respond]*, God of faithfulness, hear our prayer.

- God of justice and peace, we pray for the world you have given us as our home. We pray too for our leaders that they may have wisdom and govern with care for all. We pray as well for those who are sick, anxious, or filled with sorrow; for those who have no homes or jobs; for those who lack food; for those who are plagued by addictions; for those who feel unwelcome; for those caught in the tragedy of war or natural disaster. We pray . . . *[all respond]*, God of faithfulness, hear our prayer.

Most holy God,
hear these prayers as they are offered this very morning.
All our praise and petitions, our adoration, and our asking
we offer to you, our most gracious and loving God.
In the name of Jesus Christ
and in the power of the Holy Spirit, we pray.

[All respond.] Amen.

Closing Prayer and Blessing

The following prayer and blessing are led by the presider:

The Lord's Prayer

In the words Jesus taught us, we pray *[all join in]*, Our Father . . .

Closing Blessing

Let us bow our heads and pray for God's blessing:
Go in peace, love, and care for one another in Christ's name,
and may God, the God who believes in us,
the Christ who laid down his life for us,
and the Spirit who gives us breath day by day,
bless us with a gentle heart,
a discerning mind,
and a spirit eager to share God's love
both now and forevermore.

[All respond.] Amen.

Sign of Peace

Let us extend to one another the peace of Christ.

In Times of Celebration

IN THE CONTEXT OF MORNING PRAYER

Overview

One of the true pleasures in the life of Christians is gathering together to celebrate events that we cherish. As Christians, we look forward to the end of our pilgrimage on earth. When this pilgrimage comes to an end, we will live in the magnificent Reign of God, where there is no pain or sorrow—only rejoicing and celebration. However, we have foretastes of the wonderful things in store for us right now in this life. Moments such as these need to be celebrated. Whether it is a significant anniversary in the life of your church or school, family birthdays, or any other joyous event, this prayer service provides a way to celebrate the good things in life as gifts from God.

Preparation

Guide for Preparing a Reflection

If you are including a reflection after the Scripture reading, Philippians 4:4–9, give a copy of the following guide to the person who will be leading it and suggest that she or he adapt it to her or his own style and purpose:

In Paul's letter to the Philippians, he uses words of celebration quite liberally. "I thank my God every time I remember you" (1:3), "Yes, and I will continue to rejoice" (1:18), and "I am glad and

rejoice with all of you" (2:17) all serve as examples of Paul's joy-filled spirit as he writes to the church in Philippi. Perhaps, with this in mind, it is very confusing to learn that Paul wrote this letter while he was imprisoned. How could Paul write such a joyful letter when he was in jail? What was the source of his happiness? Perhaps Saint Paul knew that, once his time on earth was over, he would live in a place where there are no tears and no suffering. How did he know this? He had already tasted the life that was to come. He gathered with people and celebrated the joys in life with those he loved and those who loved him. He celebrated faith in Jesus with others who shared that faith. Such celebrations provided Paul with hope for the life to come.

Preparing the Music

When choosing the gathering song for this service, choose something that is familiar to all and easy for everyone to join in singing. The following selections can be found in the second edition of *Gather Comprehensive*, published by GIA Publications:
- "Sizohamba/We Will Walk With God," by John Bell
- "Canticle of the Sun," by Marty Haugen
- "We Are Marching" (South African)
- "Fresh as the Morning," by Tony Alonso
- "Halleluya! We Sing Your Praises" (South African)

Order of Prayer: In Times of Celebration

All the prayers in this service are led by the presider unless otherwise indicated.

Gathering

The presider stands and says:

> We have come this morning to celebrate _____.
> With joy and gratitude, let us stand *[motion for all to stand]* and begin our prayer. *[All make the sign of the cross.]* God, come to my assistance.

[All respond.] Lord, make haste to help me.

> Glory to the Father and to the Son and to the Holy Spirit.

[All respond.] As it was in the beginning, is now and will be forever.

Gathering Song

The person leading song invites the assembly to join in singing the gathering song.

At the conclusion of the song, all sit. If necessary, the presider motions for all to sit.

Psalmody

After all are seated, without rushing, the cantor or choir begins the psalm. The cantor or the choir sings the verses, and the assembly sings the response. If the psalms are proclaimed, the responses can be used after each verse.

First Psalm: Psalm 63

[All respond.] "As morning breaks I look to you; I look to you, O Lord, to be my strength this day" *(Gather Comprehensive).*

After a brief period of silence following the conclusion of the psalm, the presider stands and motions for all to stand, and he or she proclaims the psalm prayer.

Psalm Prayer

Let us pray. *[Pause.]*
Lord, our God,
every good thing we have
is given to us from you.
We have placed our trust in you,
and you have not failed us.
As the light of the sun chases away
the darkness of night,
may the joy of this moment last throughout this day.
And when evening comes,
may we rest secure in your promise of care.
We pray this in the name of Jesus Christ, our Lord.

[All respond.] Amen.

After the psalm prayer, the presider motions for all to sit. Without rushing, the cantor or the choir begins the second psalm.

Second Psalm: Psalm 8

[All respond.] "How great is your name, O Lord our God, through all the earth" *(Gather Comprehensive).*

After a brief period of silence following the conclusion of the psalm, the presider stands and motions for all to stand, and she or he proclaims the psalm prayer.

Psalm Prayer

Let us pray. *[Pause.]*
On the lips of children,
you place beautiful words to praise you.
We, your sons and daughters,
are thankful for all you have done for us.
But mostly, we are thankful that you
have made us your sons and daughters
by adopting us into your Son, Jesus Christ.
May we always live in the joy of his friendship.
We ask this through our brother and friend,
Jesus, the Christ.

[All respond.] Amen.

After the psalm prayer, the presider motions for all to sit. Without rushing, the reader or readers stand to proclaim the reading from the Scriptures.

Scripture Reading:
Philippians 4:4–9

A reading from the letter of Paul to the Philippians:

Rejoice in the Lord always; again I will say, Rejoice. Let your gentleness be known to everyone. The Lord is near. Do not worry about anything, but in everything by prayer and supplication with thanksgiving let your requests be made known to God. And the peace of God, which surpasses all understanding, will guard your hearts and your minds in Christ Jesus.

Finally, beloved, whatever is true, whatever is honorable, whatever is just, whatever is pure, whatever is pleasing, whatever is commendable, if there is any excellence and if there is anything worthy of praise, think about these things. Keep on doing the things that you have learned and received and heard and seen in me, and the God of peace will be with you.

The word of the Lord.

[All respond.] Thanks be to God.

Optional Reflection

After the reading, observe a period of silence. If there is to be a reflection, the person giving it stands. If there is no reflection, after the silence, all stand for the canticle.

Canticle

As the cantor begins the canticle of Zechariah (the Benedictus), the presider and all make the sign of the cross. If this is to be read, see page 120 for a copy of the text.

Intercessions

All remain standing as the presider invites the assembly to pray the intercessions. After the reader has led the petitions, the presider concludes by offering a final prayer of petition.

Christ Jesus is the source of all life and love. Let us call out to him with confidence that he will hear and answer our prayer as we say, *Lord, let your joy fill our hearts.*

• For the Church, may it be a light that warms those in despair. We pray, . . . *[all respond]* Lord, let your joy fill our hearts.

- For the world, may all come to know the good things that wait for us in heaven. We pray . . . *[all respond],* Lord, let your joy fill our hearts.
- For artists, may their creations reflect beauty that will bring hope and give joy. We pray . . . *[all respond],* Lord, let your joy fill our hearts.
- For all of us gathered here, may the light of the Gospel shine through us, and may we be ready to tell others of our faith when we are asked. We pray . . . *[all respond],* Lord, let your joy fill our hearts.
- For our friends and family, may you keep them in your love and care through our service to them. We pray . . . *[all respond],* Lord, let your joy fill our hearts.

God our Father,
everything that is good comes from you.
You are with us in every moment of our life, and you watch over us
    with your tender care.
Keep us close to you. May we never be separated from you and always be ready to share with others that you are the source of our joy.
We ask this through Christ, our Lord.

[All respond.] Amen.

Closing Prayer and Blessing

The following prayer and blessing are led by the presider:

The Lord's Prayer

With faith in the risen Lord, Jesus, let us pray the prayer he gave to us. *[All join in.]* Our Father . . .

Closing Blessing

May the Lord bless us,
protect us from everything that is evil,
and bring us to the joy of heaven.
In the name of the Father and of the Son
and of the Holy Spirit.

[All respond.] Amen.

Sign of Peace

Let us conclude our prayer, with a sign of the peace of Christ.

In Times of Anger and Hurt

IN THE CONTEXT OF EVENING PRAYER

Overview

This prayer service provides an opportunity for prayer and reflection in times of brokenness and hurt. It may be used when disappointment, resentment, anger, or disagreement is present within a family, group, or community. It is appropriate during times when a loved one has been harmed or when vengeance or violence is occurring. Whatever the situation, this service offers the participants an opportunity to pray for and about the difficult time that they may be experiencing and to seek guidance from a God who sustains us through all circumstances.

Preparation

Guide for Preparing a Reflection

If you are including a reflection after the Scripture reading, Ephesians 4:26—5:1, give a copy of the following guide to the person who will be leading it and suggest that he or she adapt it to his or her own style and purpose:

> Paul writes to the church at Ephesus about his desire for them to live fully as forgiving people. Can we infer from this that something

in their community needed to be forgiven? Maybe they held long-standing grudges. Maybe they were divided into camps of pro and con about changes in their way of life. Are we in this story? In the fighting that happens in churches, in families, in friendships, can we somehow live forgiveness toward others, as beloved children live in love, and be imitators of God? Every once in a while, someone's story takes this turn. Every once in a while, someone in the world turns toward forgiveness rather than hatred, vengeance, violence, war. Every once in a while, the enemy receives an embrace and a welcome rather than a harsh word, a threat, or a violent response.

We live in a tense time right now, and every chance we have to live with a forgiving heart toward the pain and destruction of life opens the possibility for what happens next to be good, to be redemptive.

Preparing the Music

When choosing the gathering song for this service, choose something that is familiar to all so that everyone can easily join in singing. The following selections can be found in the second edition of *Gather Comprehensive*, published by GIA Publications:

- "Open My Eyes," by Jesse Manibusan
- "Somebody's Knockin' At Your Door" (traditional African American spiritual)
- "Turn My Heart O God," by Marty Haugen
- "Turn to the Living God," by Lori True
- "Change Our Hearts," by Rory Cooney

Additional Considerations

- Invite the participants to gather in the church narthex or to create a gathering place outside of your prayer space. If the service is held in the church, gather near the baptismal font. If the service is held in a different location, you will need to have a large bowl of water present for the gathering movement.
- This prayer service has the potential to evoke emotion in some participants. Pay attention to any strong reactions and be prepared to talk them over with the group if necessary. You may also need to follow up with certain individuals.

Order of Prayer: In Times of Anger and Hurt

All prayers in this service are led by the presider unless otherwise indicated.

Gathering

As the participants arrive, the presider invites them to gather around the baptismal font (or large bowl of water) and leads them through the following ritual:

- Dip your fingers in the water and touch your forehead. As you do so, repeat the words, "Bless my understanding so that I may be here fully."
- Dip your fingers in the water and touch your eyes. As you do so, repeat the words, "Bless my vision so that I may see with clarity."
- Dip your fingers in the water and touch your lips. As you do so, repeat the following words, "Bless my mouth so that I may speak the truth."
- Dip your fingers in the water and touch your ears. As you do so, repeat the following words, "Bless my ears so that I may hear with compassion."
- Dip your fingers in the water and touch your heart. As you do so, repeat the following words, "Bless my heart so that I may offer and accept forgiveness."

(This ritual is adapted from *Prayer: Celebrating and Reflecting with Girls,* a manual in the Voices series, by Marilyn Kielbasa [Winona, MN: Saint Mary's Press, 2002], page 21. Copyright © 2002 by Saint Mary's Press. All rights reserved.)

Gathering Song

The presider motions for the participants to process to the sanctuary or the gathering space where the service is being held and to join in singing the gathering song as they walk to the place of prayer.

At the conclusion of the song, all sit. If necessary, the presider motions for all to sit.

Psalmody

After all are seated, without rushing, the cantor or the choir begins the first psalm. The cantor or the choir sings the verses, and the assembly sings the response. If the psalms are proclaimed, the responses can be used after each verse.

First Psalm: Psalm 141

[All respond.] "Let my prayer rise before you like incense, O Lord, and my hands like an evening off'ring" *(Gather Comprehensive).*

After a brief period of silence following the conclusion of the psalm, the presider stands and motions for all to stand, and she or he proclaims the psalm prayer.

Psalm Prayer

> Let us pray. *[Pause.]*
> We call upon you, God,
>   the healer of our inner hurts,
>   frustrations, and disappointments.
> We lift our hands in prayer to you this very evening.
> Help us turn our eyes to you
>   when the anger of others comes our way.
> Let those who seek to do harm
>   confront us with kindness instead.
> Draw out of us, we pray,
>   the strength to forgive those in our lives who have caused us pain.
> Hear us, O God, when we call and cry out to you
>   in hurt and disappointment.
> Grant us the wisdom needed to live a life
>   of forgiveness and love.
> Give us the grace to seek and pursue peace at all times.
> We pray this prayer in the name
>   of Jesus Christ, our Lord.

[All respond.] Amen.

After the psalm prayer, the presider motions for all to sit. Without rushing, the cantor or the choir begins the second psalm.

Second Psalm: Psalm 51

[All respond after each verse.] "Create in me a clean heart, O God" *(Gather Comprehensive).*

After a brief period of silence following the conclusion of the psalm, the presider stands and motions for all to stand, and he or she proclaims the psalm prayer.

Psalm Prayer

Let us pray. *[Pause.]*
Stay close to us, O God, for we too have sinned.
Keep us, O Lord, from pettiness.
Help us to put away pretenses, and face each other in deep trust
    without fear or self-pity.
Help us to guard against faultfinding, ill tempers, and hasty
    judgments.
Bless us, Lord, with a clean and forgiving heart.
Cleanse us, O God, from all of our sins
and restore in us a heart
in which charity and compassion
have replaced anger and hurt.
We ask this through Christ, our Lord.

[All respond.] Amen.

After the psalm prayer, the presider motions for all to sit. Without rushing, the reader or readers stand to proclaim the reading from the Scriptures.

Scripture Reading:
Ephesians 4:26—5:1

A reading from the letter of Paul to the Ephesians:

Be angry but do not sin; do not let the sun go down on your anger, and do not make room for the devil. Thieves must give up stealing; rather let them labor and work honestly with their own hands, so as to have something to share with the needy. Let no evil talk come out of your mouths, but only what is useful for building up, as there is need, so that your words may give grace to those who hear. And do not grieve the Holy Spirit of God, with which you were marked with a seal for the day of redemption. Put away from you all bitterness and wrath and anger and wrangling and slander, together with all malice, and be kind to one another, tenderhearted, forgiving one another, as God in Christ has forgiven you. Therefore be imitators of God, as beloved children.

The word of the Lord.

[All respond.] Thanks be to God.

Optional Reflection

After the reading, observe a period of silence. If there is to be a reflection, the person giving it stands. If there is no reflection, after the silence, all stand for the canticle.

Canticle

As the cantor begins the canticle, all make the sign of the cross. For evening prayer, the Canticle of Mary is the standard canticle. If the prayer service is held later in the evening, the Canticle of Simeon may be used instead. If the prayer is to be read, see page 119 or 121 for a copy of the text.

Intercessions

All remain standing as the presider invites the assembly to pray the intercessions. After the reader has led the petitions, the presider concludes by offering a final prayer of petition.

> We come together now as a community in prayer. Let us respond to the petition by saying, *Lord, in your mercy, hear our prayer.*
>
> - For all who are hurting or grieving, we pray . . . *[all respond],* Lord, in your mercy, hear our prayer.
> - For all who do not feel loved or safe, we pray . . . *[all respond],* Lord, in your mercy, hear our prayer.
> - For all who suffer the pain of rejection, we pray . . . *[all respond],* Lord, in your mercy, hear our prayer.
> - For all who seek peace, healing, and reconciliation, we pray . . . *[all respond],* Lord, in your mercy, hear our prayer.
> - For those we have hurt and those who have hurt us, we pray . . . *[all respond],* Lord, in your mercy, hear our prayer.
>
> God of compassion and healing,
> we offer you these prayers, and the silent prayers
> that remain in our hearts,
> in the name of your Son,
> our Lord and Savior, Jesus Christ.
>
> *[All respond.]* Amen.

Closing Prayer and Blessing

The following prayer and blessing are led by the presider:

The Lord's Prayer

Often we can't find the right words, nor do we know how to pray as we ought, so hear us, O God, as we pray with the words your Son has given to us. *[All join in.]* Our Father . . .

Closing Blessing

Let us bow our heads and pray for God's blessing:
May we always live in the spirit
of love and forgiveness.

[All respond.] Amen.

May we always extend mercy
and compassion.

[All respond.] Amen.

May we always find the wisdom
to cooperate with a healing and loving heart.

[All respond.] Amen.

And may God bless us,
Father, Son, and Spirit.
Now and forever.

[All respond.] Amen.

Sign of Peace

Let us conclude our prayer with a sign of the peace of Christ.

In Times of Initiation

Overview

This service would be appropriate throughout the year when young people gather for retreats and meetings that focus on preparing for the sacrament of Confirmation. It would also be effective as a post-Confirmation prayer service at the end of the school year. It would work well during the end of the Easter season, especially around the time of Pentecost. Another use would be in early fall as a commissioning for those who are beginning new liturgical and pastoral ministries.

Preparation

Guide for Preparing a Reflection

If you are including a reflection after the Scripture reading, Ephesians 4:4–13, give a copy of the following guide to the person who will be leading it and suggest that she or he adapt it to her or his own style and purpose:

> The image Paul uses of Christ equipping the saints is a beautiful one as we contemplate our role in the life of the Church. The gifts of the Holy Spirit are many and varied. So too are the ministries of the Church. There are liturgical ministries: becoming a cantor, a lector, a greeter, or a Eucharistic minister. And there are pastoral ministries: spending time with those in hospitals, nursing homes, or prisons; serving in soup kitchens; and participating in other service projects. All of our gifts, no matter how small, can be offered to our communities to build up the Body of Christ. As we mature in our relationship with God and the Church, what gifts do we have to offer? Have we been guarding our gifts closely, or have we been giving them freely? What keeps us from giving our gifts, and how can we work to change that? How can we encourage others to give their gifts?

Preparing the Music

When choosing the gathering song for this service, choose something that is familiar to all so that everyone can easily join in singing. The following selections can be found in the second edition of *Gather Comprehensive*, published by GIA Publications:

- "Veni Sancte Spiritus," by Taizé
- "Song of the Chosen," by Rory Cooney
- "Send Down the Fire," by Marty Haugen
- "Digo 'Sí' Señor," by Donna Peña
- "Send Us Your Spirit," by David Haas

Additional Considerations

- When using this service at a Confirmation gathering, consider using some of the psalms and songs that will be used at the Confirmation Mass. This will make a strong connection to the sacrament and will also be a great opportunity to introduce some of the music ahead of time. Connect with the music minister to work out what songs will be used.
- Frequently, Confirmation sponsors are not included in pre-Confirmation gatherings that involve the entire group of confirmands. Consider having the young people invite their confirmation sponsors to a prayer service in preparation for Confirmation. Then when everyone gathers for the Confirmation Mass, the connections will be stronger because the participants will have already prayed together as a community. The same invitation could be made for a post–Confirmation gathering, emphasizing the importance of continuing the relationships between the young people and their sponsors as they continue their journey of faith. Perhaps one of the sponsors could offer the reflection at the gathering or gatherings.
- For this prayer service, the Scripture reading is scripted for three readers, but it could be read by a single reader.

Order of Prayer: In Times of Initiation

All the prayers in this service are led by the presider unless otherwise indicated.

Gathering Song

The person leading song stands, motions for all to stand, and invites the assembly to join in singing the gathering song.

At the conclusion of the song, all sit. If necessary, the presider motions for all to sit.

Psalmody

After all are seated, without rushing, the cantor or the choir begins the psalm. The cantor or the choir sings the verses, and the assembly sings the response. If the psalms are proclaimed, the responses can be used after each verse.

First Psalm: Psalm 63

[All respond.] "As morning breaks I look to you; I look to you, O Lord, to be my strength this day" (Gather Comprehensive).

After a brief period of silence following the conclusion of the psalm, the presider stands and motions for all to stand, and he or she proclaims the psalm prayer.

Psalm Prayer

Let us pray. [Pause.]
God of blessings,
source of all that is good,
we look to you to be our strength this day.
We lift up our hands in praise
as we open our hearts
to the gifts of your Spirit.
Breathe new life into us,
and quench our thirsting souls
with your love.
We make our prayer through
Christ, our Lord.

[All respond.] Amen.

After the psalm prayer, the presider motions for all to sit. Without rushing, the cantor or the choir begins the second psalm.

Second Psalm: Psalm 8

[All respond.] "How great is your name, O Lord our God, through all the earth" *(Gather Comprehensive).*

After a brief period of silence following the conclusion of the psalm, the presider stands and motions for all to stand, and she or he proclaims the psalm prayer.

Psalm Prayer

> Let us pray. *[Pause.]*
> Great is your name,
> God of infinite wisdom!
> All around us is the glory of your creation,
> the work of your hands.
> Help us to see the gifts you have blessed us with.
> Bless the work of our hands,
> that our work this day will give
> glory to you,
> and unify all of your people,
> wherever they may be.
> We ask this through Christ, our Lord.

[All respond.] Amen.

After the psalm prayer, the presider motions for all to sit. Without rushing, the reader or readers stand to proclaim the reading from the Scriptures.

Scripture Reading:
Ephesians 4:4–13

Reader 1:
> A reading from the letter of Paul to the Ephesians:
>
> There is one body and one Spirit, just as you were called to the one hope of your calling,

Reader 2:
> one Lord,

Reader 3:
> one faith,

Reader 1:
> one baptism,

All readers:
    one God and Father of all,

Reader 2:
    who is above all

Reader 3:
    and through all

Reader 1:
    and in all.

Reader 2:
    But each of us was given grace according to the measure
    of Christ's gift. . . .

Reader 3:
    The gifts he gave were that some would be apostles,

Reader 1:
    some prophets,

Reader 2:
    some evangelists,

Reader 3:
    some pastors and teachers,

All readers:
    to equip the saints for the work of ministry,

Reader 1:
    for building up the body of Christ,

Reader 2:
    until all of us come to the unity of the faith

Reader 3:
    and of the knowledge of the Son of God,

Reader 1:
    to maturity, to the measure of the full stature of Christ.

All readers:
    The word of the Lord,

[All respond.] Thanks be to God.

Optional Reflection

After the reading, observe a period of silence. If there is to be a reflection, the person giving it stands. If there is no reflection, after the silence, all stand for the canticle.

Canticle As the cantor begins the Canticle of Zechariah (the Benedictus), the presider and all make the sign of the cross. If this is to be read, see page 120 for a copy of the text.

Intercessions All remain standing as the presider invites the assembly to pray the intercessions. After the reader has led the petitions, the presider concludes by offering a final prayer of petition.

> Let us place our needs before God, who blesses us with many gifts, by saying, *Lord, hear our prayer.*
>
> - For an openness to the gifts of the Holy Spirit.
>   For the courage to use our gifts even when it is difficult.
>   For the patience to nurture the gifts we have.
>   We pray . . . *[all respond],* Lord, hear our prayer.
> - For peace between nations and religions.
>   For respect between people of differing beliefs.
>   For unity among all of God's people.
>   We pray . . . *[all respond],* Lord, hear our prayer.
> - For those who support us as mentors and teachers.
>   For family and friends who nurture our faith.
>   For all those who show us patience and love
>   on our journey of faith.
>   We pray . . . *[all respond],* Lord, hear our prayer.
> - For the ministers of our parish.
>   For our priest [priests] and our entire pastoral staff.
>   For all of our pastoral and liturgical ministers.
>   We pray . . . *[all respond],* Lord, hear our prayer.
> - For all those who suffer the pains of terminal illness.
>   For all those who experience the darkness of mental illness.
>   For all who minister to those who suffer.
>   We pray . . . *[all respond],* Lord, hear our prayer.
> - For all those who have died and gone on to eternal life in Christ.
>   For all those who mourn their absence.
>   For all those who have shown us the path of Christ, especially
>   *[mention names].*
>   We pray . . . *[all respond],* Lord, hear our prayer.
> - For all the prayers we hold in the depths of our hearts,
>   especially those we now offer aloud *[pause for prayers offered by
>   the community].*
>   We pray . . . *[all respond],* Lord, hear our prayer.

God of loving kindness,
you equip your people
with the gifts of the Spirit.
Hear the prayers we offer,
and grant us what we
need to serve your people
in faith, hope, and love.
We ask this in the name of Jesus, our Lord.

[All respond.] Amen.

Closing Prayer and Blessing

The following prayer and blessing are led by the presider:

The Lord's Prayer

Grateful for the gifts of the Spirit, let us pray the prayer Christ himself taught us. *[All join in.]* Our Father . . .

Closing Blessing

Let us bow our heads and pray for God's blessing:
May the grace of God
bless us with gifts of the Holy Spirit.

[All respond.] Amen.

May we come to know Christ
through service and ministry to
all of God's people.

[All respond.] Amen.

And may God bless all of us,
in the name of the Father, Son, and Holy Spirit.

[All respond.] Amen.

Sign of Peace

My sisters and brothers, let us go forth sharing with one another a sign of Christ's peace.

In Times of Defeat

IN THE CONTEXT OF MORNING PRAYER

Overview

At the center of the Christian message is hope. However, events throughout our life can take away hope. In other words, there are times when we feel defeated. Whether we are part of a group that has battled hard in competition and lost or whether we are weighed down by burdens, we return to the gospel message of hope. Our hope lies in this: things that look like mistakes can actually be our salvation. The cross of Christ looked like a mistake to the disciples. However, the cross ended up being the world's source of salvation. The aim of this prayer service is to restore hope in times of defeat.

human experience of disappointment. For Christians, disappointment and suffering are mysteries that we try to make sense of. Countless theories have been proposed that try to answer why disappointment and suffering exist, but the only real answer to these questions is Jesus. He loves us, and nothing can separate us from his love. In times of difficulty, we have a choice; we can either use our faith in his love or lose our faith in his love. This passage from Romans tells us that by relying on our faith, we are more than conquerors even in the midst of apparent defeat.

Preparation

Guide for Preparing a Reflection

If you are including a reflection after the Scripture reading, Romans 8:28–39, give a copy of the following guide to the person who will be leading it and suggest that he or she adapt it to his or her own style and purpose:

> Disappointments are a part of living, and they are not a very pleasant part of living. Any religious belief must be able to speak to the

Preparing the Music

When choosing the gathering song for this service, choose something that is familiar to all so that everyone can easily join in singing. The following selections can be found in the second edition of *Gather Comprehensive*, published by GIA Publications:
- "How Can I Keep from Singing?" (traditional Quaker hymn)
- "Lord of All Hopefulness" (traditional Gaelic)
- "Neither Death Nor Life," by Marty Haugen
- "With You by My Side," by David Haas
- "Let Justice Roll Like a River," by Marty Haugen

Order of Prayer: In Times of Defeat

All the prayers in this service are led by the presider unless otherwise indicated.

Gathering

Once everyone has entered the space, the presider begins with the call to prayer.

> We have come to this morning's prayer weighed down by our burdens. But the Scriptures tell us to give all of our burdens to the God who cares for us. With hearts open to God's work in our lives, let us stand and pray *[motion for all to stand]*. *[All make the sign of the cross.]* God, come to my assistance.

[All respond.] Lord, make haste to help me.

> Glory to the Father and to the Son and to the Holy Spirit.

[All respond.] As it was in the beginning, is now and will be forever.

Gathering Song

The presider motions for all to stand, and the song leader invites the assembly to join in singing the gathering song.

At the conclusion of the song, all sit. If necessary, the presider motions for all to sit.

Psalmody

After all are seated, without rushing, the cantor or the choir begins the first psalm. The cantor or the choir sings the verses, and the assembly sings the response. If the psalms are proclaimed, the responses can be used after each verse.

First Psalm: Psalm 63

[All respond.] "As morning breaks I look to you; I look to you, O Lord, to be my strength this day" *(Gathering Comprehensive)*.

After a brief period of silence following the conclusion of the psalm, the presider stands and motions for all to stand, and she or he proclaims the psalm prayer.

Psalm Prayer

> Let us pray. *[Pause.]*
> Lord, our God, you are the creator,
> lover, and protector of us all.
> Because of your greatness,
> we give you thanks and praise.
> May our songs of praise and
> our desire to thank you be pleasing to you.
> We ask this through Christ the Lord.

[All respond.] Amen.

After the psalm prayer, the presider motions for all to sit. Without rushing, the cantor or the choir begins the second psalm.

Second Psalm: Psalm 121

[All respond.] "Our help comes from the Lord, the maker of heaven and earth" *(Gathering Comprehensive).*

After a brief period of silence following the conclusion of the psalm, the presider stands and motions for all to stand, and he or she proclaims the psalm prayer.

Psalm Prayer

> Let us pray. *[Pause.]*
> Lord, our savior,
> you are our constant protector.
> When the concerns of this world are too much to bear,
> you offer us your hand to help us through difficulties.
> May our faith never be shaken.
> In times of defeat, remind us of your great love,
> and we will rise to victory.
> We ask this through Christ, our Lord.

[All respond.] Amen.

After the psalm prayer, the presider motions for all to sit. Without rushing, the reader or readers stand to proclaim the reading from the Scriptures.

Scripture Reading:

Romans 8:28–39

A reading from the letter of Paul to the Romans:

We know that all things work together for good for those who love God, who are called according to his purpose. For those whom he foreknew he also predestined to be conformed to the image of his Son, in order that he might be the firstborn within a large family. And those whom he predestined he also called; and those whom he called he also justified; and those whom he justified he also glorified.

What then are we to say about these things? If God is for us, who is against us? He who did not withhold his own Son, but gave him up for all of us, will he not with him also give us everything else? Who will bring any charge against God's elect? It is God who justifies. Who is to condemn? It is Christ Jesus, who died, yes, who was raised, who is at the right hand of God, who indeed intercedes for us. Who will separate us from the love of Christ? Will hardship, or distress, or persecution, or famine, or nakedness, or peril, or sword? As it is written,

"For your sake we are being killed all day long;
we are accounted as sheep to be slaughtered."
No, in all these things we are more than conquerors through him who loved us. For I am convinced that neither death, nor life, nor angels, nor rulers, nor things present, nor things to come, nor powers, nor height, nor depth, nor anything else in all creation, will be able to separate us from the love of God in Christ Jesus our Lord.

The word of the Lord.

[All respond.] Thanks be to God.

Optional Reflection

After the reading, observe a period of silence. If there is to be a reflection, the person giving it stands. If there is no reflection, after the silence, all stand for the canticle.

Canticle

As the cantor begins the Canticle of Zechariah (the Benedictus), the presider and all make the sign of the cross. If this is to be read, see page 120 for a copy of the text.

Intercessions

All remain standing as the presider invites the assembly to pray the intercessions. After the reader has led the petitions, the presider concludes by offering a final prayer of petition.

Christ Jesus is the source of all life and love. Let us call out to him with confidence that he will hear and answer our prayer as we say, *Lord, raise us to your victory.*

- For the Church, that it may be a source of hope for all those consumed by worry, we pray . . . *[all respond]*, Lord, raise us to your victory.
- For the world, that the dignity of all peoples will be ensured, we pray . . . *[all respond]*, Lord, raise us to your victory.
- For the hopeless, provide for them friends and guardians to encourage them in their trials, we pray . . . *[all respond]*, Lord, raise us to your victory.
- For our friends and family, once we have received your grace, may we in turn be your presence to others, we pray . . . *[all respond]*, Lord, raise us to your victory.
- For all of us gathered here, may we have the confidence that all things will work for good, we pray . . . *[all respond]*, Lord, raise us to your victory.

God of victory and strength,
we offer these prayers to you
with confidence that you will hear us.
We ask that we may also hear you.
We pray this in the name of your Son,
our Lord and Savior, Jesus Christ.

[All respond.] Amen.

Closing Prayer and Blessing

The following prayer and blessing are led by the presider:

The Lord's Prayer

Remember us, O Lord. And as we pray for your Kingdom to come, keep us ever close to your side. *[All join in.]* Our Father . . .

Closing Blessing

God of all, we come to you
seeking comfort in the face of defeat.
During times of trial, you send your Holy Spirit
to remind us that we are more than conquerors in Jesus.
Open our eyes to see the true
and lasting victory we have through your Son, Jesus,
in whose name we pray.

[All respond.] Amen.

> May the Lord bless us,
> protect us from everything that is evil,
> and bring us to the joy of heaven.
> In the name of the Father and of the Son and of the Holy Spirit.

[All respond.] Amen.

Sign of Peace

Let us conclude our prayer with a sign of the peace of Christ.

Appendix

Tools for Preparing and Planning Your Own Services

Overview

This book has attempted to address some of the significant events in the lives of young people. However, events may arise that are not addressed here. In such cases, you may wish to write your own prayer service based on the outline provided in the introduction and with the aid of the suggestions in this appendix and the accompanying handouts. The following information will assist you in planning your own prayer services in keeping with the rich tradition of the Liturgy of the Hours.

Choosing Psalms

The Book of Psalms in the Old Testament is a collection of 150 prayers that were originally sung by the ancient Israelites. These prayers are both personal and communal; they concern both those who are praying and all others. Prayed by Christ and fulfilled in him, the Psalms remain essential to the prayer of the Church. The Psalms include cries of people in their life struggles, mistakes, disappointments, oppressions, and heartaches.

When we pray to God, the psalmists tell us to bring our full selves: the rage, the misery, the questions, the anger, the joy, the thankfulness, and the exhilaration of being alive. The Psalms teach us

that nothing is to be excluded from prayer. God bears it all.

The 150 psalms can be grouped into one or more of five general categories:

- *The hymns of praise and thanksgiving* sing of God's majesty, power, and wisdom, for example, Psalms 8, 24, 47, 93, 95–99, 113–118, 136, and 150.
- *The hymns of lament or petition* include both individual and communal cries to God for help in some need, for example, Psalms 38, 51, 55, 58, 59, 74, 78, 105, and 106.
- *The hymns of wisdom* sing of Israel's insights into how to live according to God's law and what brings true happiness, for example, Psalms 1, 34, 49, 73, 112, and 128.
- *The liturgical worship psalms* are used for entrance hymns at liturgies or during worship services at the Temple, for example, Psalms 15, 24, and 134.
- *The historical psalms* sing of the great wonders God has worked throughout the history of Israel, for example, Psalms 78, 105, 106, 135, and 136.

Keep the above in mind when planning what psalms you will use in your prayer service. Musical settings of each of the psalms can be found in your parish hymnal. Choose settings that are familiar to the community or easy for the assembly to learn. All of the psalms used in this book's prayer services are available on the music collection *As Morning Breaks and Evening Sets: Psalms, Canticles, and*

Hymns for the Liturgy of the Hours. Both the music collection (G-6401) and a compact disc recording (CD-609) are available through GIA Publications (*www.giamusic.com*). Consider working with the parish music director or the liturgist to assist your efforts in choosing, planning, and preparing the music for any services you develop. This will ensure that the music selections and settings you choose are best suited (and known) to the assembly that gathers. In a case where the psalmist proclaims the psalm in spoken word, usually a verse of the psalm may be used as a response by the assembly.

Morning Prayer

The singing of one or more psalms is a central part of Morning Prayer. Psalm 63 is considered to be the traditional morning psalm. However, for Lent, Psalm 51 is commonly substituted. The liturgical season should be considered, as well as the nature of the gathering. Other choices for Morning Prayer include the following:

- Psalm 8, "How Glorious Is Your Name"
- Psalm 33, "Let Your Mercy Be on Us"
- Psalm 40, "Here I Am"
- Psalm 42, "Song of Longing"
- Psalm 47, "God Mounts His Throne"
- Psalm 66, "Let All the Earth"
- Psalm 72, "Every Nation on Earth"
- Psalm 80, "Lord, Make Us Turn to You"
- Psalm 85, "Lord, Let Us See Your Kindness"
- Psalm 93, "The Lord Is King"
- Psalm 98, "All the Ends of the Earth"
- Psalm 100, "We Are God's People"
- Psalm 118, "This Is the Day the Lord Has Made"
- Psalm 131, "My Soul Is Still"
- Psalm 138, "Lord, Your Love Is Eternal"

Evening Prayer

For Evening Prayer, Psalm 141 is considered to be the standard. It is customary to use incense as it is sung. Once again, the season should be considered. Other appropriate choices for Evening Prayer would be these:

- Psalm 4, "Lord, Let Your Face Shine Upon Us"
- Psalm 19, "Lord, You Have the Words"
- Psalm 23, "The Lord Is My Shepherd"
- Psalm 27, "The Lord Is My Light"

- Psalm 51, "Create in Me"
- Psalm 66, "Let All the Earth"
- Psalm 84, "Happy Are They"
- Psalm 91, "Be With Me"
- Psalm 104, "Lord, Send Out Your Spirit"
- Psalm 110, "You Are a Priest Forever"
- Psalm 112, "A Light Rises in the Darkness"
- Psalm 117, "Go Out to All the World"
- Psalm 118, "Let Us Rejoice"
- Psalm 121, "Our Help Comes from the Lord"
- Psalm 122, "Let Us Go, Rejoicing"
- Psalm 130, "With the Lord There Is Mercy"
- Psalm 131, "My Soul Is Still"
- Psalm 136, "Love Is Never Ending"
- Psalm 139, "Filling Me with Joy"
- Psalm 145, "I Will Praise Your Name"

Choosing Canticles

From the Latin word *canticulum,* which means "little song," a canticle is a hymnlike passage of Scripture. Canticles, technically, are poems found in the Scriptures, such as the "Blessing of Israel" in Genesis and the "Wedding Song of the Lamb" in Revelation. The Bible is replete with examples of sacred poetry. The Church uses this wealth in the Liturgy of the Hours. The great Gospel canticles found in the Gospel of Luke form the climax of the Hours in which they are found. The Benedictus (or Canticle of Zechariah) is sung daily at Morning Prayer. The Magnificat (or Canticle of Mary) occurs at Evening Prayer. The *Nunc Dimittis* (or Canticle of Simeon) closes Night Prayer and with it the Church's liturgical day.

The canticles should be sung. Musical settings for this and other canticles can be found in your parish hymnal, as well in the music collection mentioned previously, *As Morning Breaks and Evening Sets: Psalms, Canticles, and Hymns for the Liturgy of the Hours.*

Recitation of the canticles is another option (although not preferred), and therefore you may consider using a spoken version of the canticles (see handout 1, "The Canticle of Mary," handout 2, "The Canticle of Zechariah," and handout 3, "The Canticle of Simeon"). The canticles are written as an alternate reading (half the group reads one verse, then alternates with the other half of the group, which reads the second verse, and so on, until the canticle concludes).

The Canticle of Mary

The Canticle of Mary, which is also called the Magnificat, is found in Luke 1:46–55. It is Mary's great hymn of praise, perhaps composed on her journey to the hill country of Judah to visit her cousin Elizabeth, who was to give birth to John. For evening prayer, the Canticle of Mary is the standard canticle.

The Canticle of Zechariah

The Canticle of Zechariah, which is also called the Benedictus, is found in Luke 1:68–79. Zechariah was a direct descendant of Aaron and thus one of the many priests serving the Jewish people. He felt himself to be cursed, however, because he and his wife, Elizabeth, now of old age, had no children. It was while performing his priestly duties, offering incense before the evening sacrifice, that the Lord revealed to Zechariah that Elizabeth would bear him a son. From that moment on, Zechariah was unable to speak, until after the birth of John, when he spoke this great canticle.

This hymn may be divided into four sections. The first offers thanks to God, using a traditional Hebrew formula, "Blessed be the Lord God of Israel." It also speaks of the great deliverance of God's people as recorded in the holy covenant of Abraham. The hymn then specifically recalls John's role as a prophet of the Most High who will go before the Lord to prepare his way. The canticle concludes by telling of the salvation that is ours through the Messiah. For Morning Prayer, the Canticle of Zechariah is the standard canticle.

The Canticle of Simeon

The Canticle of Simeon, which is also called the *Nunc Dimittis,* is found in Luke 2:29–32. In the latter days of Old Testament history, many of the Jews saw the coming of the Messiah as a violent overthrow of oppressive forces, a powerful new reign for the Second David. It was to Simeon that the Lord promised, through the Holy Spirit, to reveal the Messiah. It is assumed that when Jesus was born, Simeon was quite old. Simeon's canticle speaks of the imminence of his death, accepted now in peaceful resignation after having witnessed the coming of salvation. The hymn deals with the image of freedom from slavery, with death as a release from a long task. If the prayer service is held later in the evening, the Canticle of Simeon may be used rather than the Canticle of Mary.

Choosing Music

Through song we are able to express our faith in a way we could not without it. For this reason, the music we sing in community must invite everyone's participation. Don't be afraid to use a few songs frequently. Knowing music by heart helps the participants truly enter into the prayer.

When choosing music, consider consulting with the parish music director for input. She or he will know the repertoire of the parish, the music that people are most familiar with. In addition, most parish hymnals have indexes for liturgical seasons and themes. These can be a quick reference when looking for songs. Whenever you are planning music, always begin with the Scriptures. The deeper your knowledge of and reflection on the Scripture reading, the more informed your choice of music will be.

Consider the following questions when planning music for the service:
• Are the participants familiar with the song?
• Is the melody easy to learn and is the range possible to sing?
• Is the song appropriate to the liturgical season?
• Is the tempo appropriate for the tone of the prayer?
• Are the words appropriate and relevant to the participants?
• Are copies of the music readily available to all?

Selecting the Scripture Reading

When choosing the Scripture reading, be attentive to the season, the group that will be present, and the circumstance or occasion that is bringing the people together. The key consideration in selecting the reading is that it connects with the theme and can inform or inspire those attending the service. When planning a prayer service, the reading from the Scriptures should never be omitted.

To find biblical passages related to a certain theme or topic, refer to a biblical commentary, a dictionary of the Bible, a Bible with a thematic index (such as *The Catholic Youth Bible*), or a concordance. Be certain to prepare readers to truly proclaim the word, not merely read words on a page.

Writing and Preparing Psalm Prayers

In ancient Israel, the Psalms brought together the deepest emotions and religious beliefs of the Jewish people. The ancient Jews poured out praise, thanks, wonder, and joy but also struggle, guilt, doubt, fear, anger, and even hatred. In the Psalms they shared everything about their life and experience with God. By praying the Psalms, we offer everything to God. Praying the Psalms helps us to be honest with God and with ourselves. The Psalms can connect intimately with the life of each person who prays them. However, to make the prayers of the Psalms our own, we sometimes have to do a bit of "translation." For example, if a psalm praises God for the sea and the sky, but you have never experienced the sea, you can still be grateful for the creation around you that you do experience. Keep the idea of translation in mind when writing the psalm prayers. Consider the following process when writing a prayer:

- Read or listen to the psalm once to get an idea of what is being said.
- Read or listen to the psalm again. The operative questions during the second reading are these:
  - How does this relate to the experience of the community that will gather?
  - How can that experience be translated into a prayer that will speak to the occasion for which the community will gather?
- After you get a sense of what the passage is saying, it is time to begin writing the prayer. The operative question is, "What does this passage make me want to pray for?" Keep in mind the prayer theme (or occasion) as well as the Scrip-

ture passage that will be proclaimed later in the service.

Review the psalm prayers in this manual for examples of well-written and effective prayers. Although psalm prayers are not a required element in the Liturgy of the Hours, they are able to collect the emotion of the psalm that has just been prayed.

Writing and Preparing a Reflection

Every reflection should connect the Christian faith with the life experiences of the community. All of us have much to share from our personal life and prayer life that will be of value to others. A willingness to share experiences will only enrich these services. Consider the following process when planning and preparing a reflection on the chosen Scripture passage:

- Read the passage once to get an idea of what is being said.
- Read the passage again slowly. The operative questions during the second reading are: "What does this passage mean? And what does this passage mean to me?" Focus on the "what" questions. For the person preparing a reflection, it would be important to explain the "what" of the passage to those assembled.
  - What did the writer have in mind?
  - What is it about this passage that makes it fit in with the rest of the book?
  - What insights can you provide the listener about the passage?
- After you get a sense of what the passage is saying, it is time to respond. The operative question is, "What does this passage make me want to pray for?" For the person preparing the reflection, this is the "so what" question. Now that we understand this passage in a new way, how does its meaning apply to us as a community, Church, or world? Use a story. Get personal.
  - How are you being challenged to live this passage?
  - Is there someone who should be held up as an example?
- Finally, we rest in God's presence. What does God say back? As we go forth to try to live this word, what is God's promise to us? It is God's

work. What does God say to us as we leave worship?

Some commonsense guidelines can help the presenter share his or her story in a way that adds to the understanding of the Scriptures.

- Be brief and to the point: remember, the community is there to pray and reflect.
- Talk without preaching.
- Be realistic: talk about struggles, triumphs, and growth.
- Do not mislead the participants into thinking that you have all the answers.
- Be honest and sincere.

Writing Intercessions

The general intercessions have a threefold shape. First, the presider invites us to pray. Second, a reader announces the petition. We pray for the petition first in our heart and then by means of a response, such as, "Lord, hear our prayer." This response may be sung or recited. Third, after the final petition, the presider gathers the petitions together into a prayer, to which we all respond, "Amen."

The Scriptures play a key role in inspiring the petitions for the general intercessions. We pray for the things needed to bring us into harmony with what we have just heard proclaimed in the readings.

How do you prepare these petitions? What do you ask for? Pray for the things needed to bring us into harmony with what we have just heard proclaimed in the readings. Good petitions flow from the Scripture readings.

The Church recommends that our petitions fall into four categories:

1. Pray for the needs of the Church. For example, you might pray that we become what the Scripture readings call us to become.
2. Pray for the world and its leaders. For example, you might pray that peace and justice come to all nations.
3. Pray for those who suffer from injustice and oppression. For example, you might pray for those who may be currently suffering from a flood, a war, or an epidemic.

4. Pray for the needs of those gathered for this particular service. Create meaningful and fresh prayers of the faithful that truly represent the faithful's prayers.

A very effective approach for writing intercessions is to provide the writers with a Bible and newspaper and ask them to make a connection between the Scripture reading, the theme you have selected, and the needs of the world today.

Setting the Environment

The right environment helps a community pray well. Although prayer can take place anywhere, it is aided by a prayerful setting. The parish church is the ideal space for conducting these prayer services. A chapel or prayer room can be a good location as well. Praying involves our entire being—body, mind, and spirit. Whenever and however possible, create a multisensory environment for prayer. The use of banners, plants, candles, flowers, artwork and meaningful symbols, incense, and burning candles can enhance the prayer space.

Choose objects or decorations appropriate to the theme and useful for settling the participants into the mood of the prayer service. While planning, consider these questions:

- Is the space the right size?
- What objects or artifacts will set the right tone?
- What sounds will enhance the prayer?

Standard Materials

To save time, consider gathering frequently used materials in bins and storing those bins in a place that is accessible to all prayer leaders. Here are some recommendations for what to include:

- a Bible
- hymnals or songbooks
- baskets
- candles and matches
- a variety of colored cloths
- a variety of symbols (a crucifix, icons, photographs, and so forth)
- incense
- flowers and plants

Additional Considerations

- The Lord's Prayer should *always* be prayed by all. If you choose a sung setting, it must be one that is well known by the assembly. Reciting the Lord's Prayer tends to work the best in this regard.
- The final prayer and blessing may be sung or recited.
- The prayer ends simply, with the community sharing the sign of peace. No final song or hymn is needed.

Additional Resources

Print Resources

- *Liturgy with Style and Grace*, revised edition, by Gabe Huck and Gerald T. Chinchar (Chicago: Liturgical Training Publications, 1998).
- *Morning and Evening,* by Joyce Ann Zimmerman and Kathleen Harmon (Chicago: Liturgical Training Publications, 1996).
- *Praise God in Song: Ecumenical Night Prayer,* edited by John Allyn Melloh and William G. Storey (Chicago: GIA Publications, 1982).
- *Sing a New Song: The Psalms in the Sunday Lectionary,* by Irene Nowell (Chicago: Liturgical Training Publications, 1993).

Web Sites

www.LiturgyHelp.com
This comprehensive range of liturgical resources is designed to assist the key ministries in the parish to better prepare for liturgy and to integrate liturgy into their diverse ministries. *LiturgyHelp.com* provides cost-effective resources to individual ministers or a complete suite of Web services to parish communities and ministry teams. Resources include sacramentary texts; the official lectionary; Catholic NRSV Bibles and concordances; artwork; sample homilies; Scripture commentaries; music and psalm suggestions; and an in-depth search function for finding Scripture, music, reflections, and artwork for various events, occasions, topics, and themes. Log on to *www.LiturgyHelp.com* for more information.

www.HymnPrint.net
This new service from GIA Publications is a groundbreaking tool that brings you the convenience of downloading hymnal selections and reprint boxes of your favorite hymns and songs right onto your own computer. With *www.HymnPrint.net* you can search for the perfect song by keyword, title, composer, and other criteria. Then you're able to preview the selection in notation or text-only formats, listen to accompaniments, and download your selections.

www.liturgyhours.org
This Web site offers daily printouts of the Liturgy of the Hours Morning, Evening, and Night Prayers in Adobe Acrobat format, plus Night Prayer in Spanish, Portuguese, French, and Italian. The prayers are available in booklet formats for recitation or chant by prayer groups, and in a standard format for users who prefer enlarged text or who have mobile devices.

liturgyny.Catholic.org
This site, provided by the Liturgy Office of the Archdiocese of New York, gives additional information on how to use the Liturgy of the Hours.

The Canticle of Mary

Side 1: My soul magnifies the Lord,
and my spirit rejoices in God, my Savior.

Side 2: All people now will call me blessed,
for he has loved the lowliness of his handmaid.
The Almighty has shown me great favor,
holy is his Name.

Side 1: His mercy extends through generations,
toward those who revere him.
He has revealed his arm in power,
scattering the proud in their own conceit.

Side 2: He has dethroned the powerful,
and lifted up the lowly.
The famished have been filled with his bounty,
the rich have been sent away empty.

Side 1: He has always helped Israel, his servant,
true to his loving kindness,
just as he promised our fathers,
to Abraham and his descendants for ever.

All: Glory to the Father and the Son
and the Holy Spirit.
As always before,
so now and evermore. Amen!

(From *Liturgical Music* [St. Meinrad, IN: St. Meinrad Archabbey, 1967.]
Copyright © 1967, St. Meinrad Archabbey, St. Meinrad, Indiana. Used
with permission.)

The Canticle of Zechariah

Side 1: Blessed be the Lord God of Israel,
for he has visited and redeemed his people,
and has raised for us a horn of salvation
in the house of David, his servant.

As he promised throughout past ages,
in the words of his holy prophets:
deliverance from our enemies,
and from the control of our oppressors.

Side 2: He has shown his kindness to our fathers,
remembering always his holy covenant.
The oath sworn to Abraham, our father,
he has renewed for us,

so that freed from the clutches of our foes,
we may serve him without fear,
becoming holy and just in his sight
the rest of our days.

Side 1: And you, child called 'prophet of the Most High,'
will go before the Lord, to prepare his ways,
bringing his people knowledge of salvation,
through remission of their sins.

Side 2: For the love of our compassionate God,
as the Orient on high has shone upon us
to illumine the darkness and dispel the shadow of death,
to direct our steps along peaceful ways.

All: Glory to the Father and the Son
and the Holy Spirit.
As always before,
so now and evermore. Amen!

(From *Liturgical Music* [St. Meinrad, IN: St. Meinrad Archabbey, 1967.]
Copyright © 1967, St. Meinrad Archabbey, St. Meinrad, Indiana. Used
with permission.)

The Canticle of Simeon

Side 1: Lord, now you let your servant go in peace;
your word has been fulfilled:

Side 2: My own eyes have seen the salvation
which you have prepared in the sight of every people:

Side 1: A light to reveal you to the nations
and the glory of your people Israel.

All: Glory to the Father and the Son
and the Holy Spirit.
As always before,
so now and evermore. Amen!

(From *Christian Prayer: The Liturgy of the Hours* [Boston: Daughters of
Saint Paul, 1976], page 1013. Copyright © 1976 by Daughters of Saint
Paul. Used with permission.)

Morning and Evening Prayer Planning Guide

When planning Morning or Evening Prayer, you may find the following order-of-service planning worksheet useful. Complete the worksheet as you choose the psalm and Scripture readings and as you select or write the psalm prayers, intercessions, and final prayer and blessing. On completing the worksheet, you will have a detailed order of service.

Title or theme :

Date:

Time:

Location:

Order of Prayer

gathering song:

First psalm:

Psalm prayer:

Second psalm:

Psalm prayer:

Scripture reading:

Optional reflection:

Canticle:

Intercessions:

The Lord's Prayer:

Closing blessing:

Sign of peace:

Worship Aid Template

Order of Prayer

Gathering Song

Psalmody

    First Psalm
    Second Psalm

Scripture Reading

Optional Reflection

Canticle

Intercessions

    Our response will be . . .

Closing Prayer and Blessing

    Lord's Prayer

    Closing Blessing

    Sign of Peace

Indexes

Thematic Index

See the contents for page references to each prayer service.

In Times of Newness

the arrival of a new member of the group
the beginning of a new year, a new school year, or
   simply a new day
a new family member or the birth of a sibling
the blending of families
Morning Prayer during the Easter Season
new friendships or relationships (for example, a
   girlfriend or a boyfriend)
a new home
a new job
a new marriage

In Times of Crisis

a crisis of faith
the loss of industry, such as that resulting in loss of
   jobs
natural disasters (hurricane, fire, tornado, earthquake, and so forth)
times of civil unrest or times of terrorism
unexpected death, injury, or illness
when harm has been done to an individual or a
   community (for example, a school shooting,
   looting, violence)

In Times of Remembrance

All Hallows' Eve
All Saints' Day
All Souls' Day (*Día de los Muertos*)
American Indian Day
the anniversary of the death of an individual
Black History Month
Independence Day
Memorial Day
Rosh Hashanah
September 11
a time of remembrance of all friends and family
   members who have died
Veterans Day
Yom HaShoah (day of remembrance for Holocaust
   victims)

When Peace Is Needed

Domestic Violence Awareness Month
Human Rights Day
Martin Luther King Jr. Day
racism and prejudice in our communities
times of war and conflict on a national or international level
when seeking inner peace
World Day of Prayer for Peace

In Times of Anxiety and Worry

"fitting in" worries
mid-term or final exams week
preparing for the ACTs or SATs
relationship concerns
taking a driving exam
when applying to and waiting for acceptance from
    colleges
when young people are overwhelmed with making
    class and activity choices for the following year,
    usually in late winter or early spring

In Times of Success and Rejoicing

accomplishing an important goal
getting a driver's license
getting a first job
graduation
making the team, honor society, school musical,
    band, chorus, dance team, or various school
    organizations and clubs
surviving a serious personal struggle, illness, or
    injury

In Times of Thanks

American Indian Day
birthdays or births
college acceptance
Earth Day
Father's Day
good grades
Grandparents' Day
International Women's Day
Mother's Day
National Hispanic Heritage Week
personal, family, or communal times of celebration
Teachers' Day
Thanksgiving Day
when prayers have been answered or blessings
    bestowed

When Healing and Forgiveness Are Needed

Advent
Ash Wednesday
Domestic Violence Awareness Month
Lent
times of family strife
times of reconciliation with friends or parents
Yom Kippur

When Hope Is Needed

consolation in times of suffering
difficulties with schoolwork
times of despair
uncertain times in the life of a young person (such
    as when awaiting college acceptance)
unexpected tragedies

In Times of Transition

beginning of the school year, particularly freshman
    year
the blending of families
changes in parish or group leadership
a major move to a new home, town, or school
a new marriage
senior send-off to college, the military, or into the
    workforce

In Times of Mission

Catechetical Sunday
National Make a Difference Day
the start of a service project or a mission trip
when a congregation is responding to the needs of
    the church or the community

In Times of Celebration

an anniversary in the life of a church or a school
birthdays
a celebration of friendship
Christmas
Cinco de Mayo
college acceptance
community or church awards
Confirmation
feast days
Friendship Day
getting a driver's license
graduation
Homecoming
Kwanzaa
Las Posadas
New Year's
pay raises
Prom
registering to vote
Saint Nicholas's Day
Saint Patrick's Day
scholarships
sports awards
a team win
World Youth Day

In Times of Anger and Hurt

Domestic Violence Awareness Month
when a loved one has been harmed
when disappointment, resentment, anger, or
    disagreement is present within a family, group,
    or community
when vengeance or violence occurred or is ongoing

In Times of Initiation

a commissioning for those who are beginning new
    liturgical and pastoral ministries, usually held in
    early fall
a Confirmation retreat or a rehearsal
the end of the Easter Season, especially around
    Pentecost
a post-Confirmation prayer service at the end of
    the school year
a retreat or a meeting that focuses on preparing for
    the sacrament of Confirmation
welcoming new community members

In Times of Defeat

failing to make the team, win the game, pass the
    test, make the honor roll, get a job, pass a
    driving exam, make state or regionals, get
    accepted at a college or a university, get an
    acceptable grade on the ACTs or SATs
unfair or unjust situations

Seasonal Index

Month	Event	Service (see contents for page references)
January	the beginning of a new year	In Times of Newness
	World Day of Prayer for Peace	When Peace Is Needed
	Martin Luther King Jr. Day	In Times of Remembrance
		When Peace Is Needed
	Respect Life Sunday	In Times of Remembrance
		When Hope Is Needed
	Souper Bowl of Caring	In Times of Mission
	National Migration Week	In Times of Remembrance
February	Black History Month	In Times of Remembrance
	Chinese New Year	In Times of Newness
		In Times of Celebration
	Mardi Gras	In Times of Celebration
	Ash Wednesday	When Healing and Forgiveness Are Needed
	World Day of Consecrated Life	In Times of Mission
March	International Women's Day	In Times of Thanks
	Saint Patrick's Day	In Times of Celebration
	vernal equinox, spring begins	In Times of Transition
	National Volunteers Week	In Times of Mission
	Death Penalty Abolition Day	When Peace Is Needed
		In Times of Anger and Hurt

April	Passover	In Times of Remembrance
	Easter Season	In Times of Newness
	Earth Day	In Times of Thanks
	Yom HaShoah	In Times of Remembrance
	Pentecost	In Times of Initiation
	sacrament of Confirmation	In Times of Initiation
May	Memorial Day	In Times of Remembrance
	National Day of Prayer	When Hope Is Needed
	Cinco De Mayo	In Times of Celebration
	Holocaust Remembrance Week	In Times of Remembrance
	Mother's Day	In Times of Thanks
	Pentecost	In Times of Celebration
	Teachers' Day	In Times of Thanks
	World Day of Prayer for Vocations	In Times of Mission
June	graduation	In Times of Success and Rejoicing
	final exams week	In Times of Anxiety and Worry
	end of the school year	In Times of Success and Rejoicing
	Prom	In Times of Success and Rejoicing
	Father's Day	In Times of Thanks
July	Independence Day	In Times of Celebration
		In Times of Remembrance
August	college or military send-off	In Times of Transition
	Friendship Day	In Times of Celebration
	International Forgiveness Day	When Healing and Forgiveness Are Needed
September	a new school year	In Times of Newness
		In Times of Transition
	minister commissioning	In Times of Mission
	Catechetical Sunday	In Times of Mission
	September 11	In Times of Remembrance
	autumn equinox, fall begins	In Times of Thanks
		In Times of Transition
	American Indian Day	In Times of Thanks
		In Times of Remembrance
	National Hispanic Heritage Week	In Times of Thanks
		In Times of Celebration
	Rosh Hashanah	In Times of Remembrance

October	Make a Difference Day	In Times of Mission
	Homecoming	In Times of Celebration
	World Youth Day	In Times of Thanks
		In Times of Celebration
	Domestic Violence Awareness Month	When Peace Is Needed
		In Times of Anger and Hurt
	Yom Kippur	When Healing and Forgiveness Are Needed

November	*Día de los Muertos*	In Times of Remembrance
	Veterans Day	In Times of Remembrance
	Human Rights Day	When Peace Is Needed
		When Healing and Forgiveness Are Needed
	All Saints' Day	In Times of Remembrance
	Thanksgiving	In Times of Thanks
	Black Catholic History Month	In Times of Remembrance

December	mid-term exams week	In Times of Anxiety and Worry
	World AIDS Day	When Hope Is Needed
	Las Posadas	In Times of Celebration
	Kwanzaa	In Times of Celebration
	Christmas season	In Times of Celebration

ACKNOWLEDGMENTS

The scriptural quotations contained herein are from the New Revised Standard Version of the Bible, Catholic Edition. Copyright © 1993 and 1989 by the Division of Christian Education of the National Council of the Churches of Christ in the United States of America. All rights reserved.

The psalm refrains contained herein are from *Gather Comprehensive,* first edition, by GIA Publications (Chicago: GIA Publications, 2004). Copyright © 2004 by GIA Publications. The English translation of the Psalm Refrain for Psalms 51, 131, and 138 are from *Lectionary for the Mass* © 1969, 1981, ICEL, Inc. The refrains on pages 86, 87, and 93 are from verses and music © 1991, OCP Publications, 5536 NE Hassalo, Portland, OR 97213. Refrain © by ICEL, Inc. Psalm 40 refrain on pages 76 and 82 are from Verses and Music © 1991, OCP Publications Text © ICEL, Inc. All rights reserved. Used with permission.

The ritual exercise on page 92 is adapted from *Prayer: Celebrating and Reflecting with Girls,* by Marilyn Kielbasa (Winona, MN: Saint Mary's Press, 2002), page 21. Copyright © 2002 by Saint Mary's Press. All rights reserved.

Handout 1, "The Canticle of Mary," and handout 2, "The Canticle of Zechariah" are from St. Meinrad Archabbey's *Liturgical Music* (St. Meinrad, IN: St. Meinrad Archabbey). Copyright © 1967 St. Meinrad Archabbey, St. Meinrad, Indiana. All rights reserved. Used with permission.

Handout 3, "The Canticle of Simeon" is from *Christian Prayer: The Liturgy of the Hours,* by Daughters of Saint Paul (Boston: Daughters of Saint Paul, 1976), page 1013. Copyright © 1976 by Daughters of Saint Paul. English translation of *Nunc Dimittis* by the International Consultation on English Texts (ICET). Used with permission.

During this book's preparation, all citations, facts, figures, names, addresses, telephone numbers, Internet URLs and other pieces of information cited within were verified for accuracy. The authors and Saint Mary's Press staff have made every attempt to reference current and valid sources, but we cannot guarantee the content of any source, and we are not responsible for any changes that may have occurred since our verification. If you find an error or have a question or concern about any of the information or sources listed within, please contact Saint Mary's Press.